From KINGS *to* CLASS ACTIONS

From KINGS *to* CLASS ACTIONS

The Untold History of Collective Power and Rising Justice

TROY IAN HOFFMAN

From Kings to Class Actions: The Untold History of Collective Power and Rising Justice
Copyright © 2026 by Troy Ian Hoffman

All rights reserved. No part of this publication may be reproduced, stored in a retrieval system, or transmitted in any form by any means, electronic, mechanical, photocopy, recording, or otherwise, without the prior permission of the publisher, except as provided by USA copyright law.

This volume utilizes single quotation marks when the words are not a direct quote, when the word(s) roughly are associated with a third party or to indicate a non-agreement with the terminology, but needs it to be referenced. This is a common writing approach in legal advocacy.

No patent liability is assumed with respect to the use of the information contained herein. Although every precaution has been taken in the preparation of this book, the publisher and author assume no responsibility for errors or omissions. Neither is any liability assumed for damages resulting from the use of the information contained herein.

Published by Forefront Books, Nashville, Tennessee.
Distributed by Simon & Schuster.

Library of Congress Control Number: 2026900131

Print ISBN: 978-1-63763-435-6
E-book ISBN: 978-1-63763-436-3

Cover Design by Jensen Creative Media Group
Interior Design by PerfecType, Nashville, TN and Jensen Creative Media Group

Printed in the United States of America

The rights of the several persons may be separate and distinct, yet there must be a common interest or a common right, which the bill seeks to establish or enforce. As an illustration, bills have been permitted to be brought by the lord of a manor against some of the tenants, and *vice versa*, by some of the tenants in behalf of themselves and the other tenants, to establish some right—such as suit to a mill, or right of common, or to cut turf. So by a parson of a parish against some of the parishioners to establish a general right to tithes—or conversely, by some of the parishioners in behalf of all to establish a parochial modus.

Smith v. Swormstedt, U.S. Supreme Court, 1853

> The storyteller makes no choice
> Soon you will not hear his voice
> His job is to shed light
> And not to master.
> Robert Hunter, "Lady with a Fan," 1977

DEDICATION

I dedicate this book to all the steadfast and hard-working litigators on both sides of the aisle that protect our freedoms by striving to ensure that our legal system is fair and equitable for everyone who are endowed by the Creator with life, liberty, and the pursuit of happiness.

CONTENTS

Introduction 11

PART 1: OLDE ENGLAND
From Medieval Church Courts to the High Seas: The Roots of Group Representation

Chapter 1: 1606–1616: When the King Saved Equity! 21
Chapter 2: 1199: Rector Sues His Parishioners 39
Chapter 3: 1309: The First Judicially Created Consumer Class Action 49
Chapter 4: 1612: *Case of Sutton's Hospital* 59
Chapter 5: 1676: *Brown v. Vermuden*—Binding Absent Parties 73
Chapter 6: 1762: A License to Wage War 81

PART II: THE NEW WORLD
From Revolution to Equality: Class Actions, American Style

Chapter 7: 1820: General West and the Licentious Republic 95
Chapter 8: 1820–1845: Joseph Story Teaching America Equity 113
Chapter 9: 1845: *Smith v. Swormstedt*—The South Secedes 125
Chapter 10: 1920: The Tribe of Ben-Hur 135
Chapter 11: 1905–1925: Gilded Age Union Wars 149

Chapter 12: 1936: The Birth of Grandfather 23 — 167
Chapter 13: 1940–1950: Due Process Trumps Racially Restrictive Covenants — 177
Chapter 14: 1954: *Brown v. Board of Education* — 191
Chapter 15: 1961: The One-Way Intervention Controversy — 203
Chapter 16: 1966: The Year Everything Changed — 211

PART III: THE FUTURE

From *Mullane* to the Great Technological Threat: Group Representation Protecting Our Freedoms

Chapter 17: The World of Group Litigation: Prologue to the Future — 229
Chapter 18: Freedom Threatened — 241
Chapter 19: Keeping Freedom Alive — 249

Acknowledgments — 261
Notes — 263
Bibliography — 269

INTRODUCTION

We always head into the future from the learning and experience of the past.

Troy Ian Hoffman
January 2020

In January 2003 I drove three days from my native Florida to Southern California. I arrived just in time to experience my first sunset over the Pacific Ocean. I was pursuing an opportunity to build a class-action administration company. You know, the kind of company that sends out postcards or emails to potential class members; purchases advertising to alert the public about pending class actions; gives people a chance to opt out or leave the lawsuit; advises potential members how to file and evaluate a claim; and handles a ton of other responsibilities.

I'm sure you've received a few.

Along this almost two-decades-long ride, I realized how much there is to learn about not only administrating class actions but also about this legal procedure's long evolution. This fascinating exploration led me to the earliest 'group representation' cases, reaching back to the Middle Ages in England and other wild stories of yore that I found along the way.

The stories I discovered and now share for your enjoyment unknowingly laid the groundwork for my life and, more importantly, helped bring greater accountability to both business and government. The concepts in these tales, which go back eight hundred years, reach back and leap forward through each chapter to show the integration of litigation and legal theory that brought us to the modern-day class action lawsuit.

LEARNING FROM THE PAST

A society must know its past to guide its future. How can we best tap our potential without understanding our previous experiences? We must understand the legal, cultural, psychological, and relational circumstances that created the rules we now operate in. The only way to do that is to explore their history. So in each story I spend time discussing the era, the people, the issues of the day, and the general relevant conflicts of the time.

Over the years I've spent a lot of time with lawyers who spend more than fifty hours per week in the class action world. Very few (if any) of them know the history behind their shared professional passion or how centuries-old context informs their decision-making today—even though their decisions, and those of the judges, ultimately affect millions of consumers, stockholders, businesses.

Humans have always existed in groups. Groups have always had leaders. Group members have always known who their leaders are.

Part of human existence is conflict, followed by attempting fair ways to resolve those conflicts. More people, more conflict. And when we have conflict, humans are further compelled to appoint leaders. Sometimes these conflicts become violent (chapter 11, "1905–1925: Gilded Age Union Wars"); sometimes they are prelude to major, years-long conflicts (chapter 9, "1845: *Smith v. Swormstedt*: The South Secedes"); sometimes they arise from disputes between parties divvying up the booty of war (chapter 6, "1762: A License to Wage War").

This storybook examines moments in history when whole groups were either suing someone or being sued by someone. Because of the issue of *numerosity*, a few stand in for the many. That is, the people involved in the suit represent all the people who were harmed. Today we call those people 'class action representatives.'

These tales are not intended to be a deep dive into exact legal history in every way. They are meant to be accurate, easy to read, and digestible so that people at all levels can absorb and understand this major legal instrument that is used today in powerful ways that shape our world.

The interwoven, disparate tales you are about to read are each part of a greater tapestry, ultimately threaded by recurring legal concepts and rules that have guided group representation litigation throughout the centuries. For more than eight hundred years, the same questions arose: How do groups sue? How does an individual sue a group? Who must be included in the lawsuit? When can the lawsuit proceed without all the necessary parties? Human experience mirrors the past with adaptations for confronting the present.

These group representation stories tell tales, not just cold facts and law. I was searching for a fun way of learning so everyone—attorneys and laypeople alike—could appreciate how these complicated legal terms and concepts originated.

Be prepared to ride through history and experience the famous, the infamous, and the sometimes-little-known events that have shaped our modern legal landscape. Sometimes it is quite remarkable that one person, or a small group of people, can impact so many millions upon millions. We all impact each other in various ways. This storybook endeavors to capture the lives of some of those people and the legal principles created by their efforts to achieve justice.

THE ROLE OF EQUITY

Through the ages, kings, judges, and courts have been forced to disregard the rules of law and procedure to resolve legal disputes involving lots of people. Blow past all these rules and call it equity. Equity could be considered exceptions to the law when the result of the law is overly harsh or unfair. You might consider equity as the strong call for flexibility when established rules simply do not provide justice.

Class actions strive for equity. They seek fair judicial resolution of disputes regarding vast numbers of class members that common lawsuits are ill-equipped to administer. This book presents the best stories of the past eight hundred years about the great quest for equity and fairness.

As we embark on this history of class action adventure, we will travel from 1199 to 1966, and then take a trip into the future. We'll start in England before the American Revolution and then move on to the New World. Equity is the common thread throughout—the intertwining of approaches around *group representation* legal thinking.

As we go, you'll see a common question throughout history: Are class actions the fairest way to decide legal disputes when lots of parties with similar and/or varying interests are involved? The best way to start that discussion about equity is to tell one story out of chronological order. So chapter 1 will present a tale from the seventeenth century that contains both an initial discussion about the history and meaning of equity and a look at the evolution of the judicial procedures surrounding equity. Then we'll jump back in time for chapter 2 and follow history's journey in order from there.

HISTORIAN HOBBYIST

As a kid growing up, I was incredibly lucky. On family vacations my parents would literally stop at every museum and point of interest on the road. Then, as we drove away, they'd quiz my younger brother, Zach, and me to see if we learned anything.

In elementary school I devoured history books. My first fascinations were about Stonewall Jackson, Davy Crockett, and Sir Francis Drake. As I grew older, Lincoln, Churchill, and Nixon became my favorite reads due to my grandmother Ann, aka GaGa, who had a fantastic passion for reading and history. She motivated me to devour biographies like crazy. She had traveled the world, interviewed two presidents, written for magazines, and built a huge clothing company from scratch.

Once in high school, my fascination turned to the titans of industry, the great entrepreneurs: Carnegie, Rockefeller, Ford, Edison, J. Paul Getty, Armand Hammer, to name a few. The actions of this entrepreneurial class are the subjects of chapter 11, "1905–1925: Gilded Age Union Wars," and chapter 15, "1961: The One-Way Intervention Controversy."

The Olde England chapters travel back and examine the lives of kings, ministers, judges, cardinals, and other highly placed individuals, along with palace intrigue and the role of the church in English law. The American experience is much different, molded by revolution, drifting into civil war, the excesses of capitalism, seeking to create a better class action order, and our sad history of racial discrimination. America created or developed the class action issues of ascertainability, due process, and 'opt out' that unknowingly steered my ride in the class action administration business.

We're still figuring things out today. I founded Simpluris, Inc., my class action administration company, in 2007. In that time, I've seen how each of the more than ten thousand class action and group representation cases we've processed have had their own story, each with its own outcome having an impact on society. Some will argue that this has been for the good, some for the bad. Yet that is and has been the struggle of our justice system: to achieve fairness in all things.

WHAT HAVE I LEARNED?

As I wrote this book, I'll admit my head was spinning while learning about *res judicata*, diversity jurisdiction, necessary parties, binding absent parties, due process, and so on. I *thought* I knew and understood them. Yet, in this process, I found the basic definitions never truly encompassed the complex reality of dealing with these words in different settings, cases, and disagreements. I can at least now say that I understand them better than before.

I also learned that the legal system is not as clearly defined as I thought it was—that it is evolutionary in nature and relates almost entirely to the times and the people involved. I discovered that how things get settled is based on existing belief systems, and sometimes 'how things were just always done.' Often, but not always, the history of laws is about judges trying to be fair.

These great legal tools permit for the David-versus-Goliath-style cases that could never, as a practical matter, be individually litigated on their own. They've created a framework for social change that has helped unite a sometimes divided nation. They've instructed courts to act when the executive branch or the legislature is unable or unwilling to do so. I find all that so fascinating, and I think you will too.

I'm not an attorney; I am just a guy who happened to be in an industry that processes these class action cases at the back end for the genius attorneys on both sides of the aisle. They are the ones arguing, debating, and litigating on behalf of their parties. My perspective has always been limited.

I'm also not a historian; I am simply passionate about learning and understanding the world in which I'm involved. Along the way, I've stumbled upon all these great, little-known stories about the history of class actions.

At Simpluris, we started writing long-form blogs about cases and the history and stories behind them as an extension of our search engine optimization. In the process, the vastness and personal details of these famous cases—the icons, how they intersected with one another, their struggles in tackling tough legal issues, and the outcomes of these legendary cases—were revealed. The more we wrote, the more we realized the history of group representation was far more fun and interesting than I had ever imagined and made me curious enough to even pontificate about the future. The result: wonderfully interesting stories that I have the unique privilege of imparting to you.

Have fun and enjoy the journey back in time!

Part 1
Olde England

From Medieval Church Courts to the High Seas: The Roots of Group Representation

Chapter 1

1606–1616: When the King Saved Equity!

That we also may be like all the nations; and that our king may judge us, and go out before us, and fight our battles.

1 Samuel 8:20, King James Version

King James (yes, the one a Bible version is named after), the son of Mary, Queen of Scots, succeeded to the Scottish throne as an infant in 1567. In 1603 James became king of England and Ireland, ruled from 1603 to 1625. During his reign, King James's defense of equity is, and remains, one of the most important milestones shaping modern class actions, where cases are born out of equity, not law. As I'll illustrate throughout this book, equity is the body of principles guiding courts to do what is fair and right when the law cannot do so.

1 Samuel 8:20 imparts to the king, the protector of the people, the power to judge and guard equity—at least, it was supposed to be that way. Scripture and other ancient tales are littered with stories of

righteous kings making difficult decisions based on fairness, the critical component of any judicial system and, particularly, of equity. As long as there have been kings, there has been equity. It's not always (or often) seen, but it's there frequently enough to be notable and make thoughtful people ponder.

The task of defending and preserving equity was not easy, even for a king. James had to contend with the clash of a bitter political and legal rivalry between intellectual titans of seventeenth-century English jurisprudence, Sir Edward Coke and Sir Francis Bacon.

To appreciate the historical importance of these two great scholars, we must examine their rivalries—not just intellectually but also romantically. Each left behind unprecedented marks on history with accomplishments so vast that we can only humbly summarize them on these pages. As to issues of law and equity, Coke argued that judges create the common law over time, while Bacon contended that the king, the source of all power, had ultimate authority over judges, courts, and legal determinations.

I am told that every law student in England and America since the seventeenth century is at least made aware of Coke's *Reports*, establishing the practice of relying on 'legal precedent' instead of generalized learning and reason. Coke was Queen Elizabeth's attorney general and was appointed as chief justice of Common Pleas and King's Bench by King James.

Bacon is known as the father of modern empiricism, the theory that all knowledge is derived from sense-experience. He developed the empirical scientific method for experiments and was considered the most encyclopedic mind of his time. Bacon also served as King James's attorney general *and* lord chancellor.

Any history of written laws must surely begin in ancient Mesopotamia and Babylonia. These cultures practiced an early model of the equity rules, codified by King Hammurabi in 1754 BC. Abraham of Ur, the common patriarch of Judaism, Christianity, Islam, and other ancient Hebrew cultures, brought similar teachings from the great Babylonian empires to the Holy Land. His descendants updated and refined the concepts of equity and justice based on practical experience, wisdom, and religious principles. These are revealed in the abundant stories and teachings of the Old Testament. For instance, 1 Samuel 8:20, quoted at the start of this chapter, refers to Samuel's warning upon hearing of the Israelites' desire for kings to judge and protect them. Here, the prophet's message is simple: Be careful what you wish for.

That's always good counsel.

Fast forward to AD 313, when Roman Emperor Constantine converted to Christianity. Within ten years, the emperor's newfound faith was ordained as the official religion of the crumbling Roman Empire. Scholars tell us the Code of Canon Law is essentially based on old Hebrew legal doctrines, softened by Christianity and made more orderly by Roman practicality.

The Barbarians destroyed the Roman Empire, leaving the Catholic Church as the principal and, in some cases, sole repository of learning in the Western world throughout medieval times. Indeed, from the time of Emperor Constantine onward, bishops served as the chief arbiters of the law within their diocese. They provided a legal constant, a civilizing influence of Roman law and equity on new legal systems emerging in European kingdoms, including England.

Before we dive deep into the development of the English court system and equity, let's divert for some fun and discuss the *romantic* battles fought between our adversaries, Coke and Bacon, and the effect it had on the struggle to keep equity alive.

Sir Edward Coke's achievements in legal scholarship are so vast that to provide a complete overview would distract from our story. Anyone who performed even 5 percent of Coke's achievements would be historically noteworthy.

He was admitted to the bar in 1578. In 1581 he was the prevailing counsel in *Shelly's Case*, creating a rule regarding real property transfers. This rule is still applicable in some U.S. states and Canadian provinces, and it remains part of law students' standard curriculum.

Shelly's Case was a complicated, no generation skipping in trusts case. If one tries to convey some interest in property arising in the future to heirs of the grantee, property is the grantee's, not the heirs.

In 1592, at age forty, Coke was appointed solicitor general by Queen Elizabeth. In 1593 he was elected speaker of the House of Commons, holding both posts simultaneously. In 1594 he was promoted by the queen to attorney general for England and Wales. All of this was by the time he turned forty-two. He racked up even more legal and career achievements for another thirty-five years thereafter!

In 1598 Coke's first wife died. By all accounts it was a good marriage, and they were in love. But our legal scholar spent little time mourning. He quickly trained his eye on a beautiful twenty-year-old widow, Lady Elizabeth Hatton. Hatton was the lively granddaughter of Queen Elizabeth's prime minister and widow to the heir of the lord chancellor. She hailed from a powerful family and had immense wealth.

Sir Francis Bacon and Lady Hatton were cousins. In 1597 Bacon was queen's counsel, her principal legal advisor. In his late thirties Bacon had not yet been married, and like Coke, he had his eye on Lady Hatton. Some historical sources cite a short courtship before Coke's intrusive interloping. Political intrigue followed, as both Coke and Bacon sought their influential connections, using cunning and guile to convince the powers that be that they were the more worthy candidate to marry the wealthy and beautiful Lady Hatton.

Coke was the victor in the romantic rivalry, and he married Lady Hatton. Ironically, it is said that Bacon's brilliance is what cost him her hand. The bride's family members were concerned that Bacon's additional prestige, power, and money would dominate the clan.

For her part, Lady Hatton did not wish to marry either of these gentlemen. Coke was considered particularly boring. She found him arrogant, only interested in the law, and wholly uninterested in things she valued, such as plays or parties.

At this time, the Church of England mandated that impending marriages be announced during church services on three consecutive Sundays. The marriage ceremony had to be held in church during regular canonical hours with witnesses present. These mandates were sometimes ignored, but the requirements still existed. And the punishment for violating them was serious, including possible 'greater excommunication,' which would deprive the violator not only of church membership but also of all property, all human intercourse (talking to anyone), and possible imprisonment.

The Church took marriage and the wedding ceremony very seriously, and it did not hesitate to enforce its policies.

Lady Hatton was not at all happy about marrying Coke, and she therefore refused to suffer the complete embarrassment of a public wedding. She would only agree to a secret, clandestine wedding. Obviously, Coke was humiliated beyond words, but he needed to complete the nuptials to seal the deal. As a student of the archbishop of Canterbury at Cambridge, Coke figured he'd take his chances and agreed to a private marriage ceremony.

The archbishop was enraged. A prosecution for greater excommunication ensued. Coke, Lady Hatton, her father, and the priest were all defendants. Coke, the nation's attorney general, pled ignorance of the law—an obvious anomaly as he was known far and wide as the most knowledgeable and respected lawyer of his time. Ignorance of the law is never considered a valid defense. If it was, how could any law ever be enforced?

Shockingly, the defense was successful, making this the last historical recording of a successful ignorance of the law defense. How Coke managed to pull it off is unknown to this day.

The newlyweds had nothing in common. Marriage to Coke was an obvious demotion in Lady Hatton's social standing. She never changed her name to Mrs. Coke. Retaining the Lady Hatton moniker was a lasting insult to Coke. However, a year later, the stork brought the couple a daughter, whom they named Frances.

As our story unfolds, the history of Coke v. Bacon's personal, professional, and intellectual rivalry has overwhelming implications on the development of the role of equity in our modern legal system. Hence, to appreciate the high levels of intrigue to follow, some foundational understanding of the development of the English court system is important. So, for just a moment, let's turn back the calendar six hundred years.

Before and after the AD 1066 Norman conquest of England, the king was considered the "fountain of justice" and power, taking the necessary steps to do the right thing when ordinary avenues of legal respite were ineffective. At that time, there was little in the way of judicial precedent, few statutes, and no intermediate appeals court.

King Henry II ruled England from 1154 to 1189. His closest confidant was Thomas Becket, who had returned from studying Roman law at the University of Bologna, the leading educational institution of its day. Becket was Henry's chancellor, essentially second in command to the king. He is credited with creating the first national court system in England encompassing a single body of law. Written procedures were adopted along with the institutionalization of juries. This was all part of a program to consolidate power to the king, along with a strategic program to instill power to traveling royal judges, called 'judges in eyre.' These judges traveled the kingdom and dispensed justice in the name of the king, usually following the edicts of the king's chancellor.

Over time, the resolution of some legal issues became routine. Rules were written down and became the early foundation of English common law. With the formalization of legal procedures, Chancery became a court of equity. Chancery grew and obtained more cases as it met a discernable, judicial administrative need. Common law courts had many deficiencies. They were slow, overly technical, and refused to hear various forms of testimony that were not compelled. To make matters worse, they were often controlled by powerful litigants. Most importantly, common law courts possessed no power to grant specific relief to prevent a threatened, future wrong. Today, courts routinely exercise their authority to issue these injunctions.

Of course, common law judges were obviously unhappy and resented the competition and the overruling of their perceived jurisdiction by judges who disregarded the usual rules of law and procedure. The rise of Chancery also had its effect on group litigation, the forerunner of the modern class action. The common courts were unable to handle the larger issues that these more complex cases presented. Group litigation required *extraordinary jurisdiction*, creating the *rule of necessary parties* legal doctrine and carving out an exception for these cases.

Necessary Parties: Any party whose interests may be affected by the outcome of a lawsuit, but whose absence prevents complete judgment on all issues. However, a court can decide between the existing parties. This concept will arise frequently in the group litigation context.

Fast forward and returning to the times of Coke and Bacon, the two dueled on great issues of legal procedure: how the rules of the game were written. In 1592 Bacon was thirty-one years old. In the

House of Commons, he proposed a plan to amend, consolidate, and condense the entire body of English laws. His aim was to reduce it in bulk, simplify it in form, render it consistent, and leave out all repetitions and whatever else was obsolete. Writing an actual code, or rule book, is a process called *codification*.

Coke, who was nine years older than Bacon and a member of Parliament, was at the height of his political power and near the peak of his fame. Bacon's proposition was completely averse to Coke's fundamental common law approach to the administration of justice.

Common Law is law derived from judicial decisions as opposed to constitutions or statutes.

As a scholar in the world of politics, Bacon was distrusted, a view enhanced by the novelty of his proposition. As a politician, Coke was immeasurably superior. Bacon's codification effort in England fell, stillborn. But it attracted marked attention abroad, accelerating the development of the civil law system on the continent that already possessed a strong foundation of Roman law.

In 1606 Coke was appointed chief justice of the Common Pleas Court. Chancery started issuing injunctions halting plaintiffs' collections of money judgments in Coke's common law courts grounded on the precept that an injustice would result if the judgments were enforced. Common law judges felt disrespected. Their judgments were summarily overruled. Chief Justice Coke forced the issue, seeking supremacy for his common law court and the precious common law itself, a direct challenge to His Majesty the King's almighty Chancery jurisdiction.

King James saw himself as an absolutist, above the courts, the source of all law. In 1610 Archbishop Bancroft, the chief overseer of the King James Bible, recommended that the king have the privilege of judging whatever cause pleased his own person, free from all risk of prohibition or appeal. James summoned the judges to his council and asked whether they consented to this proposal.

Coke replied,

> God has endowed your Majesty with excellent science as well as great gifts of nature; but your Majesty will allow me to say, with all reverence, that you are not learned in the laws of this your realm of England, and I crave leave to remind your Majesty that causes which concern the life or inheritance, or goods or fortunes of your subjects are not to be decided by natural reason, but by the artificial reason and judgment of law, which law is an art which requires long study and experience before that a man can attain to the cognizance of it.[1]

King James flew into a rage. "Then am I to be *under* the law—which it is treason to affirm?"

Coke replied, in Latin, "King ought not be under man but under God and law."[2]

In James's view, judges were officers of the Crown, and the courts could be used for his political ends. The king appointed all the common court judges and could dismiss them at will. Coke, believing in an independent judiciary, opined that the king's privilege was subject to legal limitations. Of course, the common law judges agreed with Coke.

In 1613 Bacon was appointed as King James's attorney general. He had the king's ear—and a plan: Judges should be directed to postpone arguments and decisions on public interest cases until the king's 'pleasure' was known. Predictably, the king was keen on this idea. Bacon went to work. The king would be supreme over all judges and courts, the way it should be for a king. Bacon reasonably saw Coke as an obstacle to this plan.

Chief Justice Coke's court, Common Pleas, was the target of Chancery's injunctions. Bacon recommended that King James 'promote' Coke to chief justice of the Kings Bench directly concerned with matters of interest to the king's policies and away from the direct line of fire of Chancery's injunctions.

The king agreed.

Coke wasn't thrilled with the move as it reduced his legal influence. To rub salt into the wounds, the new position paid Coke significantly less. Bacon always sought ways to lessen Coke's influence. This battle would not go away easily.

Bacon finally saw his opportunity in 1614. He commenced a monumental project to codify the common law, which he had attempted to do twenty-two years earlier as a young member of Parliament in 1592. Once again, Coke defeated Bacon's grand proposal. But Bacon's efforts, as stated earlier, accelerated the inception of a movement in Europe to do so, finalized after Napoleon conquered Europe, which remains the basis of civil law on the continent to this day. It is amazing—one group turned down a transformational idea while another group adopted and embraced it.

But never fear, in 1615 Coke came up with his own idea. He declared Chancery's injunctions void based upon a 1392 statute designed to limit the jurisdiction of papal courts.

But . . . weren't they both courts of the king? How could one court limit the other?

King James was not at all amused.

In 1616 Coke forced the common law versus equity dispute to a final resolution. He announced that any lawyer running off to Chancery to stay the execution of a common law judgment would forever be barred from presenting cases in King's Bench Court, his jurisdiction.

So, say you're a barrister. You're told never to come to an important courthouse ever again if you file an injunction request in Chancery

Court, even once. The interests of your client be damned. The king and Chancellor Bacon were not happy.

Coke upped the ante and poured fuel on the fire. Some plaintiffs wanted their money and disregarded the Chancery injunctions. The chancellor locked them up for violating the injunction. Coke issued their release from jail under habeas corpus. Obvious tension and drama were at play. Bet the barristers were chatting this one up when taking a pint after a day in court.

King James created a commission to study the matter. His Majesty's Commission determined with great fanfare: Yes, Chancery is correct; the king is indeed supreme over the common courts. In a surprise move, the king accepted absolute power over the courts. Okay, this was not really a shock; in fact, it was a decision that surprised absolutely no one.

King James heartily endorsed the commission's report. After all, he was king.

During a trial that took place shortly afterward, Bacon wrote the judges that it was "his Majesty's express pleasure the farther argument of the said cause be put off till his Majesty's farther pleasure be known upon consulting him."

In other, more modern terms: "I am the king. You must listen to me."

In a reply, drawn up by Coke and signed by the other judges, the king was told, "We have advisedly considered of the said letter of Mr. Attorney, and with one consent do hold the same to be contrary to law, and such as we could not yield to by our oaths."

James was incensed, furious about this turn of events. He summoned all the judges, including Coke, to the palace at Whitehall. A royal tongue lashing for the ages awaited. James asked, "In a case where the king believes his prerogative or interest concerned requires the judges to attend him for their advice, ought they not to stay proceedings till his Majesty has consulted them all?"[3]

Translation: When the king is interested in the outcome of the case, hit the pause button so the king's views are heard and strongly considered.

All the judges except Coke answered, "Yes! Yes! Yes!" They fell to their knees before the king, shaking and praying. With heads bowed and hands laced in prayer, they beseeched the king, begging for his forgiveness and pardon. But Coke responded, "When the case happens, I shall do that which shall be fit for a judge to do!"[4]

King James considered Coke's response disgraceful and insolent. But Coke maintained at least enough of King James's respect to stay on the job. King James clearly had some serious management issues.

Bacon had finally won a round against Coke. The king saved equity! He decreed that the state's interest in assuring fairness in the legal system was paramount when common law rules failed to do so. The Chancery courts could maintain their injunction power over the common courts, and Coke could no longer restrict counsel utilizing this powerful equitable procedure.

From this singular moment, we can take a giant leap across centuries of legal developments and declare that this is why modern-day lawyers can bring class action lawsuits.

As you will read in chapter 10, "1920: The Tribe of Ben-Hur," this exact procedure was utilized to *halt* a massive class action in America. But this saga is far from over. Bacon advised James to suspend Coke from the Privy Council, akin to our modern-day cabinet, and to dismiss him as chief justice at the King's Bench Court. Coke was removed from the Privy Council, but James was still not ready to terminate Coke from the bench—for the moment.

Translation: "Sorry, but whatever the king wants is not the law."

Enter George Villiers, later to become the Earl of Buckingham. By 1616 this young man had been dubbed the "Gentleman of the Bedchamber," and then "King's Master of Horse." As a fine dancer, swordsman, and entertainer, he gained social access to the king, quickly becoming James's new royal favorite. How favorite was he? When the closeness of their relationship was discussed within the Privy Council in 1617, King James advised:

> You may be sure that I love the Earl of Buckingham more than anyone else, and more than you who are here assembled. I wish to speak in my own behalf and not to have it thought to be a defect, for Jesus Christ did the same, and therefore I cannot be blamed. Christ had John, and I have George.[5]

While Coke was still hanging on as chief justice of the King's Bench in 1616, he was urged by the king to appoint Villiers for the newly opened chief clerkship position at the court. Justice Coke refused. That was the last straw. King James removed Coke from the court for insubordination, a profoundly serious and dark blow to Coke's professional and social standing.

In 1618 George Villiers, the Earl of Buckingham, urged King James to appoint Francis Bacon as lord chancellor. By 1619 the then-Duke of Buckingham had gained appointment as Lord High Admiral of England, seemingly a better post than head clerk at King's Court. Personally, I would rather be an admiral than a clerk.

Buckingham made many requests for favors from Bacon, who obliged. In time, some saw those actions as corrupt. Formal charges later came back to haunt them both, as we'll see in chapter 4, "1612: Case of Sutton's Hospital."

Former Justice Edward Coke saw his power waning. His marriage to Lady Hatton, as expected, did not go well. They appeared to the world on decent terms but hardly even lived together. Through Lady Hatton's troubles, she found a strong consoler, counselor, and friend—Chancellor to the King Francis Bacon. A path to reacquiring royal acceptance then fell into Coke's lap. Duke Buckingham's eldest brother, Sir John Villiers, was attracted to Coke's fourteen-year-old daughter, Lady Frances. However, he was poor and in his early forties. He also had what was described as an 'uncertain personality.' Coke realized that his standing in royal circles could be revived with a previously unknown political asset, his daughter.

Coke had previously slighted Buckingham by denying him the lead clerkship in King's Bench. Now Buckingham was more powerful. Coke sorely needed to restore his position to good graces again. Without consulting Lady Hatton, he cut a deal to 'sell' his daughter's hand in marriage to Sir John, who didn't have much money, at least in royal terms.

But Lady Frances loathed Sir John.

The teen girl pleaded with her parents to never even mention marriage. Lady Hatton was more than displeased; she was furious. Mother Hatton ran off with daughter Frances in the middle of the night, hiding in the home of a friendly cousin (an earl, of course).

Coke was enraged by his wife and daughter's defection. He applied to the Privy Council for a search warrant, but Bacon sat on the Council and delayed its immediate issuance. The folk history of the time implied that Bacon was actively involved in the sleuthing required to hide Lady Frances. Coke was not to be deterred. Clad in light armor and weapons, the recently defrocked chief justice of England rode off with various armed men and servants. He learned of his wife and daughter's whereabouts. In the king's name, he broke down one locked door after another. He finally found his sought-after family members hiding and cowering in a closet. Poor Lady Frances was whisked away to meet her fate after an emotional and physical tug of war between mom and dad.

Fresh from the fight, Lady Hatton raced to London in hot pursuit of Coke's raiding and kidnapping party to free her daughter. A wheel of her carriage broke down on the way, ending the hot pursuit. Once again on the road, she sought Chancellor Bacon's assistance, going directly to his home. Bacon's doorkeeper informed her that the chancellor was ill and indisposed. She was not to be denied. While sitting in the parlor and as the servants were entering, she slipped her way into his sleeping quarters, much to Bacon's surprise and embarrassment. Lady Hatton was beside herself and a nervous wreck. Bacon tried his best to console her.

Chancellor Bacon, because he detested Coke and because of his friendship with Lady Hatton, devised a quick plan to prosecute Coke for *riot* in the Star Chamber, the highest criminal court of that day in England. Utilizing his high governmental post, he also wrote Buckingham and the king (who was in Scotland) that the match was imprudent for reasons of state.

Buckingham advised Bacon not to be too alarmed. The king's response was even stronger, writing Bacon from Scotland, rebuking him for not considering the "riot and violence of them that stole away Coke's daughter." The king was more concerned about providing for his favorite Buckingham, whom he had told the Privy Council that he loved, than in limiting Coke, the king's grand and perpetual thorn from many years prior, when his majesty was saving equity for us present-day mortals and commoners.

Bacon saw which way the wind was blowing. He halted the Star Chamber prosecution against Coke and ordered Lady Hatton into strict confinement. Bacon needed to convince Lady Hatton to stand down on her opposition to the marriage.

Lady Hatton finally wrote the king from confinement, agreeing to the marriage and cooperating on issues of land transfers. The king personally arranged the marital settlement of lands and walked the bride down the aisle on Michaelmas Day. Lady Hatton was still confined and did not attend the wedding. However, soon after the marriage, she was set free and held a grand party with the king and queen in attendance. Her husband, Edward Coke, however, was not even invited.

> **Michaelmas Day** was widely celebrated on September 29, near the equinox as darker and colder nights arrived in England. Saint Michael was an important angelic warrior protecting against evil forces that grow stronger in the dark months.

The marriage between Lady Frances and John Villiers was worse than awful. Calling it a disaster would be an understatement. By 1620 Sir John's mental illness had become complete. He had lost all reason. By 1621 Frances deserted him and started living with another man. She gave birth to a son in 1624, followed by an adultery conviction. Frances was sentenced to do penance, required to suffer the indignity of sitting in front of her house dressed only in a loin cloth. However, she escaped prison by bribing the jailkeeper and dressing as a boy on her way to Paris to avoid serving the sentence. The king issued a warrant for her arrest, sent through diplomatic channels to France. The case had various post-conviction challenges, and it appears the final record of the resolution, if any, no longer exists.

Although Lady Frances's relationship with Coke was always quite strained, she did care for her father during his last year of life.

King James ruled until his death in 1625.

Buckingham had many failed military and diplomatic campaigns. Parliament tried to impeach him twice. King James dissolved Parliament on both occasions to prevent the proceedings from advancing. The king's favorite was stabbed to death in August 1628 by a disgruntled army officer who had been passed over for promotion after being wounded in battle. Due to public dislike of Buckingham, this assassin was deemed a hero in many circles. When his body was placed on public display in Portsmouth, it became an object of veneration.

James's son, Charles I, arranged for Buckingham to be buried in Westminster Abbey.

Francis Bacon held the lord chancellor post until 1621. During the four years that he was chancellor, he cleared off the long backlog of his predecessor, passed judgment in thirty-six thousand cases, presided over the House of Lords, was active in all affairs of state, participated in all manner of social functions, and added largely to his voluminous writings, most of which were translated into Latin, either by himself or by others under his supervision.

Bacon's grandest scientific achievement, *Novum Organum*, is considered the starting point of modern science and fostered the paradigm shift that led to the modern scientific revolution. We'll see more about this grand work in chapter 4, 1612: "Case of Sutton's Hospital." He has been attributed by some to writing a few of William Shakespeare's plays.[6]

Edward Coke penned, "Every man's house is his castle."[7] More importantly, he led the parliamentary passage of the Petition of Right, placing English liberty upon an indestructible foundation. It is considered one of the three crucial constitutional foundations of England, along with the Magna Carta and the 1689 Bill of Rights. Coke opposed the king's billeting soldiers in private homes without the owner's consent and was an early embracer of the notion that no man should be twice punished for the same offense, which was incorporated into the Third and Fifth Amendments to the U.S. Constitution, the Bill of Rights.

Coke's lifelong adversary, Francis Bacon, even wrote, "Had it not been for Sir Edward Coke's Reports (which though they may have errors, and some peremptory and extrajudicial resolutions more than are warranted, yet they contain infinite good decisions and rulings over of cases), for the law by this time had been almost like a ship without ballast; for that the cases of modern experience are fled from those that are adjudged and ruled in former time." Coke laid the groundwork for the modern case method.

Lady Hatton and Edward Coke never reconciled after the Lady Frances debacle. At his funeral she remarked, "We shall never see his like again, thanks be to God."[8] She probably wasn't the only person happy to never see his like again. His persistent use of torture over decades to extract criminal confessions would appear anathema to his legal, scholarly ways.

American lawyers still follow English common law principles, protected by Coke, alongside rules of equity, protected by Bacon and King James.

The U.S. Constitution mandates that federal courts have jurisdiction in both law and equity. Chapter 8, "1820–1845: Joseph Story Teaching America Equity," examines this U.S. Supreme Court icon. He exerted his gifted mind to influence federal equity, which was somewhat repugnant to the fresh and practical minds of the new nation. It can be said that equity survives in America today thanks to King John and Francis Bacon.

As you will discover in forthcoming chapters, the development of group representation/class action law followed a rather organic and circuitous path. While its origins seemed at first pinned to the vagaries and whims of a king seeking to maintain power over the centuries, the wisdom of balancing the law and equity resulted.

Chapter 2

1199: Rector Sues His Parishioners

The church used to send a minister to lead prayer every day. And now, the priest only presides over burials in Barkway. If we wish to bury our dead here in our home, Nuthampstead, the priest refuses to preside, but still demands payment. Its four miles round trip to Barkway to bury and visit our dead.

—Unknown fictional Nuthampstead parishioner, 1199

The Archbishop of Canterbury Ecclesiastical Court provides us with the first, still surviving, limited record of a group representation lawsuit, dated 1199. The documentation was found in a church basement long ago.

In the late 1880s British legal scholars and chroniclers commenced an intense historical preservation project to collect and organize ancient court documents. All that we have about *Master Martin Rector of Barkway v. Parishioners of Nuthampstead* are witness summaries that have been translated from the original Latin into English. While this is the oldest known group representation lawsuit, collectively suing groups of people had been occurring for some time before 1199.

Rector Martin hailed from Barkway, England, a tiny village three-quarters of the way to Cambridge from London. This small community's history reaches back to Saxon times, but it has always been a sleepy hamlet. For a time, Barkway was known as the coaching stop where horses were changed between larger urban centers. When the Barkway stop was terminated in the 1880s, the small town became an even quieter backwater.

Today only eight hundred people live there. There are no businesses or commercial services—not even a 7-Eleven. St. Mary Magdalene Church dominates the town. Construction on the present building commenced about eight hundred years ago, but the continuous Christian presence—first Roman Catholic and then the Church of England, or Anglican Church—has been present in Barkway for over a thousand years.

Martin's parishioners, the 'group,' were domiciled in Nuthampstead, an even tinier hamlet, almost two miles from Barkway, currently home to only 150 residents. The village has a nice pub restaurant, which is open about four days a week. A local Nuthampsteadian told my researcher that a small church was constructed there in about 1850, but it hasn't been used since 2000. It was recently sold and converted into a residence.

A crucial component of this case was who was made to traverse the often sloppy and wet two miles of road between these two exceedingly small English towns, and when. Paths and roads, crisscrossing between homes, farms, and other small towns, were, of course, unpaved and often filled with mud. Traversing this type of road is never fun unless you are in a four-wheel drive vehicle, and those weren't readily available eight centuries ago. In fact, only a few of the 1199 Nuthampstead parishioners even owned horses.

The parish was the basic unit of medieval ecclesiastical organization. Nuthampstead has been in the religious parish of Barkway for over a millennia and remains so today.

Rector Martin sued four of his parishioners as representatives of the remainder of the flock. Martin asserted his right to ask for and receive customary burial fees as payment for providing funeral services. This seems completely fair; everyone should expect fair payment for their professional services. Rector Martin, however, refused to officiate burials taking place in Nuthampstead—although he still demanded payment for those burials taking place without him.

So the parishioners had to choose between burying their loved ones in Nuthampstead with no priest or burying them in Barkway with Rector Martin officiating. But whatever they chose, Martin had to be paid.

The Nuthampstead parishioners protested Martin's decision to make Barkway the official cemetery for their parish. Traveling two miles in those conditions was a serious trek—not just for a funeral service but every time a family member wanted to visit their loved one's grave. Imagine plodding and squishing down a muddy path in the rain for two miles and back every time you wanted to honor your grandma!

The community of villagers also had another gripe, which we would today call counterclaims. They did not appreciate the fact that neither Rector Martin nor his priests ever visited Nuthampstead during the week as their former clergy had done.

In our modern times, a pastor taking the audacious step of prosecuting his congregation would automatically terminate the ministerial relationship. Why would the flock of faithful ever again seek spiritual guidance from someone who was suing or had sued them? The answer lies in the innately communal medieval English social structure. Since authorities in this time period did not possess the administrative apparatus to enforce obligations individually, instead they did so collectively.

Vicars of Barkway, Hertfordshire, England, eleventh to twenty-first centuries.

The *frankpledge* was a program instituted by King Canute II the Great of Demark and England (1016–1035) compelling groups to be accountable and responsible for their own behavior. It required males aged twelve and over, regardless of whether they were free or serf, to be located within a local governmental unit, paying a surety to assure the observance of laws and the collection of taxes. The rich and the clergy were excused from this obligation.

The entire group was responsible for the good conduct of all members. This shared compulsory responsibility of mutual protection was enforced to prevent crime among their members and ensure that the taxman was always paid.

The higher powers needed a responsible representative of the group with whom they could communicate concerning these matters.

How the duties and/or punishment were meted out for failing to uphold these responsibilities was frequently left to the groups themselves, with no common standards from one community to the next. In this time, the laity of the parish was responsible for collecting tithes and offerings. Hence, Rector Martin, in 1199, sued four leaders of the congregation as the representatives of the entire group.

Since little is known about this lawsuit, my research team contacted St. Mary Magdalene Church and the Barkway City Council. They were attempting to discover whatever facts could be gathered about the structural remnants of the ancient church. We provided the good people of Barkway with a copy of the limited records of the 1199 lawsuit. Surprisingly, neither the church leaders nor a local historical group knew anything about Rector Martin's lawsuit. But being kind Christians, they volunteered the names of the prior vicars of Barkway by providing a photograph of a listing hanging on the wall at St. Mary Magdalene. Rector Martin's name is on the wall attributed to circa 1120, yet the legal scholars date the witness summaries to 1199—a difference of almost eighty years. Could there possibly have been two different Martins?

We inquired how the list on the interior church wall was formulated. With great honesty, as active church members should, particularly when it comes to matters of church affairs, they admitted to having no idea how or when the list was created or its source. We were told, "It's always been there." The ancient witness summaries reveal other priests leading the small community before Martin. Their names also do not appear anywhere on the church's present-day listing.

The ancient witness summaries speak of the customs of the priests ministering before Martin's time. The list on the wall states that an unknown priest predated Martin. While we have scant information about the lawsuit, we have abundant information about the customs and structure of medieval life in rural English villages. Regardless of the times, it is always a complicated affair whenever numerous parties are involved in a legal dispute. Or, to state it plainly, it can get really messy when a lot of people all start suing at one time. However, in the early days, no one raised any concerns about numerosity or necessary parties. Society had already collected itself into well-defined and cohesive groups.

Numerosity refers to the impracticability of bringing all members of a group or class into the lawsuit (legal term "joinder") as parties. Today federal courts presume numerosity with groups of forty or more.

Medieval group litigation was quite different from modern-day class actions. Today litigants rarely know each other. This 1199 case, in contrast, occurred within the confines of a small village and included people attending the same church (the *only* church). Considering how small Barkway and Nuthampstead are today, it can safely be presumed that these tiny hamlets were even more quaint way back when. Today people learn of a pending class action from a postcard notice; in 1199 Nuthampstead, however, everyone knew each other.

"Rector Martin is suing us!" the congregants probably exclaimed as word got around the small town almost as quickly as a viral Facebook post.

Before Edward Coke institutionalized the practice of precedent, which I discussed in the previous chapter, courts made decisions based on *customary rights*—or, stated simply, "This is the way it's always been." Contrast customary rights with *prescriptive rights*, such as a statute or a contract that grants someone a particular right not previously existing. Back in 1199 and for centuries afterwards, court rulings predominantly looked to the past and considered the natural conduct of the parties involved.

We know the chapel in Nuthampstead was independent sometime before Martin began leading the flock and that there was no mother church. Years before this controversy, the chapel's patron, Sir Ralph de Noers, gave the church as a charitable donation to monks located in Colchester, about fifty miles to the east. The monks, in turn, leased it to the parsonage of Barkway, presumably Martin, for ten shillings per year—or about $2.50 in today's U.S. currency. The Nuthampstead chapel fell within Barkway parish.

One of the issues in contention was who really owed what to whom because of these transfers. During these times, a long-term struggle existed whereby smaller churches sought to obtain independent control from the great monastic houses and other large churches. It's the time-honored story of the big guy trying to control the little guy. It seems that the big church in Barkway didn't like the little church of Nuthampstead stealing its business. The Barkway church was seeking tithes and revenue by requiring Nuthampstead parishioners to attend the mother church in Barkway for big events and feasts. It is unclear why anyone would oppose attending a feast.

The good people of Nuthampstead desired daily services in their local chapel. This had always been the custom before the nobleman gifted the church to the monastery, who in turn leased it to Rector Martin, or someone associated with him. Instead of daily services, Martin sent a chaplain to lead services only three days per week. Also, the parishioners did not appreciate that Barkway had the sole right to determine in which church cemetery a deceased parishioner would be buried, or that Martin still required payment even if he or one of his priests was not officiating at the funeral.

Who wants to walk two miles for a burial or to visit the dearly departed when it's so much easier to do that right in your own hometown? Why should the Nuthampsteadians have to pay Martin or his priests for work they wouldn't do? As it was, in modern terms, the members were paying the staff and all the bills but still had to do all the dirty work themselves. It just did not seem fair.

This dispute could be deemed a religious consumer class action crossclaim against the rector/chaplain about where and how often religious services were to take place and be celebrated. The parishioners, of course, wanted the dedication of a full-time rector for their tithes, just like before. In the religion business, what could be better than a congregation desiring to gather and pray together every day? The mother church only wanted to provide a part-time priest to save money and travel time. Due to the lack of numbers, the Nuthampstead parishioners possessed limited consumer buying power.

Injustice is always present no matter what the environment or the period. In a case like this one, it might seem easy to determine right from wrong. But common villagers of that era had little power. Today class actions provide an institutional framework for righteous consumer claims. These villagers were simply seeking what had customarily been provided to them for what they had paid in the past—a good legal strategy considering the *customary rights* approach of the day. All they wanted were daily prayers, burial of their dead at home, and to not have to pay a minister who did not even show up.

The beauty of group representation litigation is that it gives voice to those who, when standing alone, could never profoundly change the way things are. As a group, as a body of people that are joined together in wanting change, they are truly able to transform their lives and the lives of those around them with real, effective reforms that alter their daily existence. At least these concerns were able to be heard in Canterbury's Ecclesiastical Courts, as religious courts must always be deemed courts of equity.

We have no idea how the Canterbury Court ruled. Like a Bob Dylan song, no information is provided at the beginning of the tale, some detail is given in the middle of the saga, and the ending is left to your imagination. As far as we know, these two little towns have always been peaceful neighbors without any notable disputes—at least since 1199, when Rector Martin stirred things up a little.

Litigation *against* groups appears to have occurred at least as far back as the time of the frankpledge and was apparently not unheard of nor that big of a deal in 1199. It has continued for the eight hundred years since, and it will keep going for a long time into the future.

Chapter 3

1309: The First Judicially Created Consumer Class Action

The islanders of Jersey and Guernsey were always jealous of their ancient privileges, and seem not at all to have liked the interposition of a permanent ruler between themselves and their sovereign. . . .

Otho on his part apparently regarded his government as a domain to be exploited. . . . The evil was increased by Otho's long absences from England, during which the deputies had to take their orders from his attornies.

—*Girart Dorens*, Sir Otho de Grandison 1238–1328, *Cambridge University Press on behalf of the Royal Historical Society, 1909*

When most people hear the name Normandy, they automatically think of the Allied invasion of June 6, 1944, to liberate Europe from the Nazis. Equally, or perhaps more importantly, was its mark on world history on Christmas Day 1066, when William the Conqueror, Duke of Normandy, the last successful hostile invader of the British Isles, was crowned Norman king of England in Westminster Abbey.

Guernsey and five other tiny Channel Islands are located about twenty-three miles off the northern French coast of Normandy. The Romans arrived at the Channel Islands about AD 56. Little is known of their presence. The Normans, descendants of the Vikings, arrived in 933 claiming the islands for the Duchy of Normandy. This early history is important for the *jurisdictional* portion of our tale, as the Channel Islands, to this day, are a unique political entity: They are part of the British Crown but not part of the United Kingdom of Great Britain. The tiny Channel Islands were part of William's Normandy realm. He brought this small group of islands along for inclusion into his new English kingdom.

In 1204, six kings and one queen later, King John, of Magna Carta fame, was forced out of Normandy by Philip II, king of France. The Islanders' loyalty, however, remained to London. In return, King John granted them a charter with a unique autonomous existence, including the authority to make their own internal decisions. Seemingly sensing the reality of the circumstances, Philip agreed that the islands would remain under the jurisdiction of the English Crown.

Despite this peace agreement, decades of conflict between the English and French kingdoms followed. Control of the Islands remained in dispute. In 1259, in one of many agreements entitled The Treaty of Paris, John's son, Henry III, and Philip's grandson, Louis IX, settled once and for all that the Islands would remain under the jurisdiction of the English Crown—and they do unto this day. The British Parliament has no say over Channel Islands affairs.

Since this is a collection of stories about group litigation, let us introduce our main protagonist for this tale, Sir Otes Grandison. Otes was born around 1238 in Lausanne, modern-day Switzerland, just north of Geneva and close to the French border. Circumstances brought him into the service of King Henry III. Sir Otes was assigned to the household of Prince Edward, Henry's son.

In 1267 Edward and Otes were victorious together in glorious battle. Henry awarded Otes prime lands by the River Thames in London. How prime? The land was located on the north side of the river between the present-day London and Millennium Bridges.

In 1271 Prince Edward, heir to the throne, led an army of the Ninth Crusade. Prince Edward and Sir Otes, now best chums, rode side by side to save holy Jerusalem for Christianity. When Edward, Otes, and their band arrived at the standard crusaders' sailing off point in Southern France to the Holy Land, they learned that most of the allied Christian forces had abandoned the fight for glory; they had settled individually with their adversaries before blood was shed. The ambitious but reasoned prince was now stuck in a quandary outside of his control or making. Returning to England would undoubtedly brand him in history as a coward and failure. He decided to continue the holy crusade with only eight sailing ships and thirty galleys (small fighting ships) filled with a scant thousand men, including a mere 225 knights.

Upon arriving at the great Roman port of Acre on the present-day Israeli coast equal distance between Tel Aviv and Beirut, our noble prince found the city under siege by Baibars, sultan of Egypt. With the arrival of the prince's small army, Baibars decided to turn away and seek lower hanging fruit. Sir Otes was quickly appointed as an executor (trustee) of Acre.

On a fateful night in June 1272, Baibars sent an assassin to Prince Edward's bedroom. The assassin held a knife laced with poison. The killer presumed that Edward was asleep. The stabbing began with an initial blow to the prince's hip. The seemingly mortally wounded prince grasped a dagger from his side table and stabbed his would-be assassin in the head. Sir Otes rushed to the scene. Immediately recognizing that the wound contained poison, best chum, honorable knight, ever-loyal Otes sucked the poison out of the wounded hip of the heir to the throne.

The prince's life was saved! It never hurts one's standing in a royal court to save the life of the future king while on crusade in the Holy Land. Increased goodwill to the *maximus*.

Soon thereafter, Edward learned that King Henry was gravely ill. Deciding to forgo any future crusading, he rushed home with Sir Otes. On the long journey back to England, Edward was informed that his father had already died. Prince Edward was now King Edward II.

Sir Otes's rise quickly followed. He held numerous military posts as the expansion of the English throne on the British Isles continued. He was also assigned to various diplomatic posts, creating cozy relationships with most leaders of Western Europe. In 1277 he was granted a lordship for life over the Channel Islands, the home of our group representation litigants.

In 1290 Sir Otes, consistent with his standing, returned to Acre as the powerful throne administrator and master of all English knights in Palestine. Thereafter, he represented England at the Papal Curia, the central governing body of the Catholic Church. Otes was now a well-connected fellow across Europe and a massively influential figure in the English royal court.

But all was not well in the lands he managed.

The Channel Islanders despised Otes with a passion. He was a tyrannical overlord, hated by his subjects because he was cruel, miserly, and without any concern for the commoners. But they challenged their immensely powerful lord anyway regarding how their taxes were to be paid. Sir Otes is either the defendant or the principal of the sued agents in our group representation lawsuits of 1309.

Modern-day plaintiffs' class action lawyers often believe judges lean toward conservative business interests. As we turn to our historic group representation lawsuits in the medieval Channel Islands, with Sir Otes as defendant, consider the stacked deck that the lowly Islanders faced. They were suing the best friend of the king, the fellow who saved his life while on holy crusade, who rose to represent England in the heart of the Catholic Church and, on the side, had been granted a life term appointment as governor of their island.

Now, let us briefly turn to a little history of legal process and procedure in early fourteenth-century England.

Before the Norman Conquest, the judicial system in medieval England centered on the king personally traveling the countryside administering justice in cities and hamlets. Later, in chapter 7, "1820: General West and the Licentious Republic," our first story about early American class actions, I will tell how U.S. Supreme Court justices traveled the *circuit*, meaning they individually traveled to different states to act as one-man federal appeals courts. The ongoing practice of traveling courts, originating in England, lived on in America until the federal circuit courts were created in the 1890s.

Back in pre-Norman England, the king was working his tail off every single day. He had a lot of land and many people to take care of, plus he had to administer justice. The king would hop on his horse with his mates and knights and ride from town to town and set up court—either in the open air or at the local castle or church. He personally listened to each case that could not be solved locally, one at a time, and he would decide. Constant work. Often he was on the road fighting battles or administering his kingdom, deciding both executive and judicial matters.

When William the Conqueror invaded England, he was simply too busy to personally act as chief justice of his new kingdom. He apparently was far better at instituting public policy than the rulers he defeated. William commenced the use of special royal commissioners to travel the kingdom in his stead to hear pleas and dispense justice. The commission was called the *General Eyre*, and it was granted wide equitable powers along with executive administrative functions. These commissions represented the person of the king. In the next chapter, we will see how Chancery courts rose with the demise of the General Eyre and took the preeminent role of equity jurisdiction in the English court system.

Our first 1309 Channel Island group representation lawsuit is *John the Mason v. Certain Bailiffs and Ministers*. Since these stories are about group representation lawsuits, John was not alone. Piers Howel, Robert the tawer, Samson Lemoeine, Andrew Lesant, and Thomas Amend on their own behalf *and on behalf of all the other tenants*, were suing Sir Otes's bailiffs and ministers. My initial reaction to reading the "on behalf of" language was that it sounded like class action representatives for cases I've administered on a constant basis for years. Their gripe? As tenants of Andrew's Wharf, St. Peter Port Parish on Guernsey, they were collectively challenging Sir Otes's outrageous order *trebling* (or *tripling*) their rents.

In case you're wondering, a *tawer* prepares leather. We know it today as a tawe. I wrote *tawer* with a small letter because that is how it appears in the case decision when stating their names. *Mason* is capitalized in the original case name.

Raymond Marcin, in his 1974 law review article "Searching for the Origin of Class Action," credits these plaintiffs, the *class action representatives*, as the possible "authors of the original class action."[9] More likely, our credited crew obtained the idea from others, but this is the oldest, still surviving recorded case using the "on behalf of others" language.

You couldn't ask for a more David-versus-Goliath confrontation than the common folk of Guernsey having the unmitigated gall to sue the powerful, wealthy Sir Otes.

Enter Sir John of Fressingfield. In 1309 he was sent by the king on a General Eyre commission to hear the *John the Mason* case. No surprise, Sir John ruled in favor of Sir Otes's ministers.

But the Islanders were still justifiably stirred about Sir Otes's ruthless rule.

Jordon Discart was the plaintiff in the second lawsuit against the oppressive Sir Otes, and hopefully, he will be deemed a hero in the annals of class action history after the expectedly wild success of this book. Jordon was the local *granger*, usually meaning he acted as a bailiff, overseeing rent and tax collection from the storehouses and barns of the lord. In this case, Jordon sold the lord's corn for local Guernsey coinage. These coins were the basis of local trade but held little value off the Island. Sir Otes insisted that all debts and rents due be paid to him in the far stronger French currency instead of the local money. This had the practical effect of tripling rents.

Sounds unmistakably similar to the *John the Mason* lawsuit.

Jordon and others sent numerous petitions to King Edward II, the new king, about these unjust matters. In turn, Edward dispatched a royal commission to sail to the Island, comprised of Sir John of Fressingfield, again, along with a Sir William Russell, to convene another General Eyre. Sir William had also previously ruled for Sir Otes on a similar matter. So the same team of judges previously ruling for Sir Otes were now weighing in on very comparable matters. From the starting gate, a favorable result for the plaintiffs seemed unimaginable.

But in *Discart v. Otes*, Jordon sought a decree, *for himself only*, that Sir Otes should accept local money as payment instead of French coins, a monetary circumstance nearly identical to that in *John the Mason*. Of course, Jordon Discart cannot be alone in his legal predicament. This is a book about groups. All the other Islanders had to pay Sir Otes in French currency for their debts and rents as well. But Jordon filed on his own behalf only—seemingly not the sort of chap inclined to fight other folks' battles.

The case took a few interesting procedural turns. Sir John and Sir William determined that they had a conflict of interest, or couldn't be fair, having ruled on the same issue for Sir Otes before. The General Eyre decided that it was best to send the case on to London and the King's Council. *These judges ordered the Islanders to choose one among them to speak for all.* The King's Council would decide and govern the judgment for everyone. The phenomenon here, at least by fourteenth-century standards, was that judges created the class because the legal system could not be forced to adjudicate the same case again and again. They would hear one giant case to settle this entire issue once and for all and be done with it.

Sir John and Sir William entered the following decree:

> The Commissioners have adjudged that these complainants must thrash this matter out with the King's Council; and, after some discussion, the complainants were told that they must appear *coram Rege Ubicunque etc.* a month after Michaelmas; and that a single complainant should argue the case for all, and that the determination of the King's Council in that one case would govern the judgment in all similar complaints.[10]

With the benefit of a quick Google search, *coram Rege Ubicunque* means *wherever the king*. Michaelmas, which I also mentioned in chapter 1, was the Christian feast held on September 29. No one wanted a court case interfering with Michaelmas celebrations.

More importantly, Sir John and Sir William, *sitting as judges, created a class action.* These fourteenth-century judges took similarly situated individuals and told them to appoint a representative of their class to argue the issue that would result in a judgment binding on all members of the class, even those unnamed and not appearing.

This is the first known instance in which a single individual went to court and the judges turned the individual proceeding into a group representation action.

Intriguing to me is the absence of discussion about notifying the other Islanders about the proceedings. Back then, most information was conveyed verbally; few could read, and it seemed that everyone else just went along for the ride. But the brilliance here is that Sir John and Sir William entered this decree to basically have one person go before the King's Council and represent the entire crew for final and complete resolution of the ongoing controversy.

When the Islanders appeared at Westminster, they lost their case before the King's Council. The oldest preserved consumer class action in history was a loss for the Islanders.

While no known record exists of the Islanders' emotions about this ruling, they must have certainly known of Sir Otes's close bonds with the past and present king. But their descendants' resolve was not dampened. Two hundred fifty years later, in 1565, forbearance finally prevailed. The Islanders sought redress to the Queens Majesty Courts, which, in turn, referred the matter to the Queen's (Elizabeth) Privy Council regarding the administration of the entire justice system on their Islands with another group representation lawsuit, *Devyke v. Petevyn*. Devyke appeared "*on behalf of* the inhabitants of the Isles of Jersey and Guernsey," seeking relief, which "*they* humbly desire."[11] More group representation.

It seems that Devyke had particularly good barristers. Instead of asserting the inequity of the excessive rents and debts, they attacked the complete arrangement of administration of justice as violative of King John II's original grant of ancient rights of locally administered justice. The Islanders' loyalty to England over France could not be forgotten. The Queen's Privy Council agreed. No longer would justice be administered from London. King John's original grant extinguished the unfair rulings of *John the Mason* and *Discart*.

[F]rom henceforth all suits commenced there already, or hereafter to be commenced between any subjects of those isles, should be heard, ordered, and adjudged in the same isles, and not within this realm. And the like order . . . should be kept in suits arising and containing two parties, whereof the one is resident here in England, and the other in the said isles. And further . . . that no appeals should be made from any sentence in judgment, given in the said isles hither but only *au roy et son counsaill* [according to the words of the charters] which agreeth . . . with such order and form as heretofore hath been accustomed. . . .[12]

Customary rights that all English subjects and agents of the Crown were similarly bound to. The Islanders won their representative action by questioning issues of procedural fairness to the entire population of the Islands. The volume of beer consumed in the Islands' pubs upon hearing the news is lost to the sands of time.

As for Edward I, he died in 1307, the last king to participate in a crusade. Popes sought to roust up another crusading army, but European kings had grown weary of wars of attrition and revenge.

Sir Otes lived until ninety years of age, passing away in 1328. Pope John XXII ordered his tomb placed in the Lausanne Cathedral, Otes's hometown.

Today Guernsey remains a British Crown dependency, with its own currency, the Guernsey pound, since 1921. Dear departed Queen Elizabeth II, William the Conqueror's twenty-sixth great-grandchild, remained the absolute ruler of the Islands, but it was just not proper for Her Majesty to exert monarchical authority.

Chapter 4

1612: *Case of Sutton's Hospital*

A hospital for the relief of the poor, aged, maimed, needy, or impotent people, and free-school for the maintenance and education of poor children or scholars.
—*"Letters Patent" from King James I to Thomas Sutton, June 22, 1611*

In the early seventeenth century, England emerged from the Middle Ages into the Renaissance. The exciting times during the events and litigation surrounding the *Case of Sutton's Hospital* propelled this period of human rebirth: The first edition of the King James Bible was published; Shakespeare authored *Henry VIII*, his last play; Galileo improved the newly invented telescope and quickly discovered that Venus circled the sun, not the earth, that Jupiter had four moons, and that the planet Neptune existed; and the first tobacco was imported from the Virginia colony.

As I discussed in the first chapter, Sir Edward Coke started compiling court opinions from across England in 1572. This work commenced the practice of legal precedent we take for granted today. Before the Coke Reports, there was little accepted practice of legal precedent, particularly on a national scale.

In this true tale, our two protagonists from chapter 1, "1606–1616: When the King Saved Equity!" are at each other's throats again. Coke was the lead judge in the case of Sutton's Hospital, a seminal legal milestone both in laying the foundation for the nascent domain of corporate law and in its effect on group litigation leading us to modern-day class actions.

Sir Francis Bacon was plaintiff's counsel, and he was also unquestionably the most renowned philosopher and scientific mind of his time. At heart, Bacon was more philosopher and scientist than lawyer or politician, so brilliant that the latter professions could almost be considered secondary to the former. But apparently they were necessary to keep our inquisitive, prolific genius busy. As every school child should know (and hopefully you are now being reminded), Bacon was the father of the scientific method. Any memories of fifth grade science class kicking in?

Bacon rose to dizzying heights in politics and law, including attorney general and lord high chancellor of England—the right-hand man to the sovereign. Bacon's brilliant writings regarding logic, entitled *Organum*, challenged the heretofore sacrosanct writings of Greek philosopher Aristotle, who lived from 384 to 322 BC. After almost two thousand years, Bacon was the first to challenge his theories. If you have the temerity to take on Aristotle, well . . .

In 1620 Bacon's *Novum Organum, sive indicia vera de Interpretatione Naturae* (New Organon, or true directions concerning the Interpretation of Nature) was published, whereby he espoused the "Scientific Method," calling usage of inductive principles and empirical data obtained through observation and experimentation the only reliable method to formulate trustworthy data upon which scientific theories and hypotheses could be based. No longer should truths of the world be predetermined by kings and their ministers. Bacon called preconceived concepts and notions "the idols of the mind."[13] We humans, Bacon professed, are inclined to jump to conclusions. An unbiased system of data collection along with inductive reasoning casts away the limitations of our minds imposed by governmental authorities, and the idols that naturally control our psyches with prejudices and presumptions. No longer could people fall back on the age-old defense, "I always thought that . . ."

Bacon's scientific method starts with a question: What do you wish to learn or discover? Then a hypothesis is formed—an educated guess of sorts. Next, you seek to prove or disprove the theory through observable experiments that can be repeated. You document and write everything down. *Everything*.

Conduct the experiments in a controlled way to ensure reliable results.

Repeat. Over and over again.

Then, finally, you arrive at a conclusion.

Never in science's lexicon had there been such a procedure. Indeed, the concept of controlling variables, such as the amounts or types of substances involved, was required. Even the time of day or ambient environment required study, control, and documentation. Then variables could be changed, one at a time. Bacon discussed the necessity of creating "Tables of Deviations." All is considered basic science today. Back then, it was considered subversive and bordered on blasphemy.

For instance, how fast does a plant grow? The answer depends on when and how often you water, the type of soil, the amount and duration of light, and the air temperature. You must keep track of everything, resulting in creating data. You find the truth by real facts, not from myths, edicts of kings and ministers, or 'they say.' Indeed, Bacon's *Novum Organum* inspired the creation of the first scientific journal. It all sounds similar to Coke's Reports on legal precedent.

I've already shown that these two great minds had a lifetime of clashes. But why?

The popular view is that Coke detested Bacon's superior intellectual abilities. Bacon was ten years younger, considered more handsome, an idealist, and funny. Coke's brilliance was the law and nothing but the law. Otherwise, he was seen as a brutish bore.

Until this time, the legal rights and claims of a community were, for the most part, collective, following the social structure of life during this period. Representatives of groups routinely appeared in court on behalf of the community they represented, without formalized or particularized approval. Hundreds of years of group litigation, the precursor to modern class actions, had taken place without consideration or any shred of concern for anything even close to the modern parameters of adequacy for a class definition, such as ascertainability, numerosity, commonality, or typicality. These issues were simply never raised.

Scholarship is unable to locate any consistent application to define an 'entity' or how a collectivized group (i.e., 'the class') was defined. Defendants never raised the issue of being sued by an ill-defined group. It simply was not an issue of jurisprudential concern during this period. Of course, this was a time when the representatives and the represented all lived closely together and everyone knew each other well, as in the case of the parishioners in Nuthampstead or the grangers on the Channel Islands.

As for adequacy of representation, these groups usually appeared without counsel by already established leaders, representing their group—whether a village, parish, borough, trade or craft guild, farmers of an area, government associations, or others. Lawyers were not always needed to speak for the group back then.

Sometimes these groups were sued collectively as defendants, simply naming a few leaders who were responsible for paying the claim. In turn, they sought reimbursement from all the members.

The leaders knew the membership of their group. Compared to our modern view, this was a very informal process.

The entrance of corporations, the new legal toy on the block, was a game changer. What was to be done with these new, formally registered groups that contrasted with historical group representation concepts? Corporations were different. At this point, there were no long-held, time-tested, working legal theories. In the *Case of Sutton's Hospital*, just trying to figure out a corporation's place in the scheme of the law alongside court management of group litigants was a daunting task.

Be prepared for Sir Edward Coke's amazing legal mind.

Edward I, the last royal crusader and good buddy of Sir Otes Grandison, as we saw in the previous chapter, ruled England from 1272 to 1307. King Edward instituted a program where his lawyers would inquire of towns, guilds, and individuals throughout the kingdom the privileges they exercised and by which right they claimed to exercise them. This was much like Bacon wanting to know the facts.

In 1345 the first explicit town charter was granted. The Crown, in granting a charter of incorporation, was erecting an entity that by guarantee would outlast not just the lives of the grantees but, more importantly, the life of the grantor, the king.

Early examples of the rise of corporations come from the Age of Exploration commencing in the sixteenth century. The sovereign granted trade monopolies to the British East India Company, the Virginia Company, and the Massachusetts Bay Company. Many other similar monopoly grants were provided for trading around the world, as well as domestically.

Corporate entity usage was in its formative stages in the early 1600s, slowly substituted in place of medieval group litigation as the defining entity for guilds, towns, villages, etc. The king provided grants for various projects, trades, and land acquisitions, and the Crown was assured that taxes would be paid in exchange for royal permission to act. The king or landlord often put a group together for its own purposes as opposed to the historical system of the group itself establishing formation.

Interestingly, towns, guilds, and other entities would frequently assert loss of ancient documents proving original grants. This was considered perfectly fine. The application of the theory was that if a group claimed prior unity and, with the passage of time, represented misplacement of core documents, they would still be considered a valid group or corporation. A dual system of legal, fictional corporations alongside collectives and the frankpledge remained in place in England until the early 1800s. Indeed, it seems that collectives, in a way, transformed into *de facto* corporations.

In the aftermath of the Reformation and the suppression of Catholic monasteries that provided charity for the poor, the English Crown encouraged secular organizations to replace this necessary social function and demonstrate that religious competitors were no longer a viable or necessary alternative. The Crown provided grants in the form of charters, or corporations, to build educational centers, hospitals, and alms (poor) houses that provided quasi-governmental benefits in the form of charity. These governmental programs were particularly popular during the Reformation. English sovereigns needed alternatives to the Catholic Church's mission to provide for the poor and unfortunate, an important royal public policy. The case of Sutton's Hospital was the early use of one such grant.

Thomas Sutton amassed his fortune as Master of the Ordnance in the North Parts from 1569 to 1594. His responsibilities included crushing rebellions and participating in the Siege of Edinburgh in 1573 to regain control from the supporters of Mary, Queen of Scots. Sutton obtained great wealth from this office, including profits from procuring military supplies and fortifications. Let's call him an arms dealer—always profitable work. He also leased coal fields and married an extremely rich widow, further increasing his fortune through money lending.

On May 9, 1611, Sutton bought the land at issue in the lawsuit for an almshouse and school. It was a formidable property, including a premier mansion. When Queen Elizabeth entered London for the first time in 1558, after ascending to the throne, she stayed there. So did her successor, James I, equity's savior, upon his arrival from Scotland in 1603.

On June 22, 1611, Sutton obtained a "Letters Patent" from King James I for a charity. His plan was to provide a hospital, chapel, school, and almshouse. An immensely wealthy merchant of Sutton's stature had little problem obtaining the Letters Patent from the king. It provided permission to found a "hospital for the relief of the poor, aged, maimed, needy, or impotent people, and free-school for the maintenance and education of poor children or scholars."

A noble mission indeed.

But the grant was vague as to the institutional or legal form of the hospital as the creation of corporations was a new practice providing ripe ground for future legal challenge. Sutton was granted power to name a "master" and a board of directors. He deeded the land to the entity and appointed a master.

Then, on December 12, 1611, Thomas Sutton died before his dream charity institution could be built.

Simon Baxter, Sutton's nephew, seeking the vast fortune of those lands, mounted a legal challenge to Sutton's will. He was an heir at law and could inherit the entire estate if his lawsuit succeeded. Baxter retained philosopher and scientist Francis Bacon, who, at the time, was England's solicitor general. Amazingly, the fact that Sutton loaned Bacon substantial sums prior to his death and was a high government official was of little concern to the seventeenth-century court. But these were different times with a vastly different set of legal ethics.

Baxter sued the board of governors in trespass. He claimed that the hospital was not properly established, and hence, the land in question should pass by operation of law to him rather than to the vaguely established corporation. A key component of that challenge was the legality, width, and breadth of the Letters Patent juxtaposed to the challenge that a corporate entity could be formed prior to its actual existence. Bacon argued for Baxter that the corporate model must be rooted in the ways of medieval times—a stunning move backward for a philosopher endeavoring to take science into the modern world.

His core argument claimed that the hospital's legal foundation failed because the incorporation preceded the granting of lands. Bacon argued that to make a grant valid, the social organism, like a guild or church congregation, must come first. Initially, establish the hospital, give the land to a master and inhabitants, and *then* seek incorporation. The social reality must precede the legal formality. Otherwise, the necessary legal formality would be an empty shell, unable to exist on its own. Bacon argued that the attempted corporation died at the instant of its birth as it lacked the sustaining social reality giving it life.

In short, Sutton's actions were backwards and hence invalid.

But the times, they were a-changing.

The medieval social model of corporations that placed great value on existing groups, where guilds and towns sought formality after already existing, was fading. Chief Justice Coke and his court were faced with a transitioning legal environment and thus forced to recognize that past precedent was based on a slowly vanishing social structure. This case also presented a less-than-clear Letters Patent and a need to interpret the role of emerging corporation law.

Scholars argue that Coke's lengthy opinion inaccurately described the prior five hundred years of group litigation to neatly fit his theory of the replacement role of emerging corporate law. Coke focused on the monopoly of the state to recognize groups, akin to modern courts granting class action certification. Coke argued that a group without a charter was suspect. But what of all the prior litigation involving groups previously deemed to validly represent their individual members that had proceeded without any charter? Coke found that they existed either by a proper legal fiction of a prescription by implied grant or by a lost charter. However, these wise scholars argued that Coke's concepts were never even discussed in any of the old cases.

In the end, the most experienced judges in England rejected Bacon's medieval view of the corporation in favor of one that a modern lawyer would recognize. The king's Letters Patent created a present corporation. This new legal form could exist in the air, awaiting the grant of land that gave it economic power. Sutton's process was correct: First create the legal forum, then endow it with wealth.

Of course, destroying a worthy charity in accordance with royal policy interests and rewarding a greedy heir seeking to obtain Sutton's wealth must have also played a role in Coke's decision.

The case of Sutton's Hospital stands as a bellwether mark of the demise of medieval group representation, as society began shifting closer to the corporate form of group representation. The corporation was a valid legal entity, its creation within the power of the king or Parliament. Groups were validly pre-ordained. Consequently, the formal creation of groups, legally recognized by charter or incorporation, was morphing away from the social reality construct of the past.

The case was decided within one year of Sutton's death, a welcome timeline for any present-day litigator.

However, for scholar, scientist, and sage Sir Francis Bacon, things did not go well.

Coke had always resented Bacon and Duke Buckingham for having him removed from the King's Bench, the same court that heard the Sutton's Hospital case. Their tight associations complicated things, as Bacon and Buckingham were close: Bacon was chancellor to King James, and Buckingham was the king's "favorite."

Coke began to plot his revenge, which would begin to reach fruition a decade after the Sutton's Hospital matter. It centered on the issue of impeachment.

Impeachment was initially utilized in England in the late fourteen century, but it fell into disuse in the mid-fifteenth century during the War of the Roses. Political disputes were resolved on the battlefield, not in the House of Commons. While Bacon was publishing his opus *Novum Organum* (while serving as chancellor to King James), Coke was researching how to reinvigorate the ancient and dormant procedure of impeachment. In 1621 Coke returned to Parliament after twenty-eight years. He sought to destroy his great rival Bacon once and for all. Coke mapped out a shrewd plan. Before seeking Bacon's impeachment, he successfully tested the prosecutorial procedure of another royal official—less than coincidentally, a relative of Buckingham.

During this time, the House of Commons was furiously convinced that judicial administration in England, across the board, was corrupt. Bacon, as Lord Chancellor, was the head of judicial administration. It was standard practice for high government officials to receive gifts from highly placed individuals, both within and without England. These gifts were made openly; nothing was secret. A strong case could be made against Buckingham corruptly accepting gifts as bribes. But, at this time, he was deemed beyond reproach, protected by King James.

Coke's case against Bacon lay in the principle that Buckingham and Bacon worked hand in hand, and as a result, Bacon was guilty of Buckingham's crimes. In 1621 the impeachment process commenced. King James needed to sacrifice Chancellor Bacon to save his buddy Buckingham. No evidence ever emerged that Bacon altered any decisions based on the gifts that he received. However, he clearly saw the writing on the wall. Coke had won. Bacon expedited the entire messy process by confessing guilt, thereby avoiding a full-blown trial in the House of Lords.

Bacon was sentenced to never again hold an official post. He was fined £40,000 and sentenced to imprisonment as determined by King James. James commuted Bacon's sentence after two days in the Tower of London and waived the monetary fine. By 1624 Bacon was permitted to resume his seat in the House of Lords, essentially erasing the terms of his punishment. But Bacon never took his seat in the chamber, pleading advanced age and infirmity. Most would say the real reason was embarrassment.

Throughout this entire episode, Duke Buckingham was not deterred or appeased by his own close call with impeachment. Indeed, during this time, Prince Charles, son of King James and heir to the throne, strongly disapproved of Buckingham's relationship with and influence over his father.

Charles also sought an alliance with the grand enemy, Spain. Charles's plan was to marry King Philip III's daughter. James was opposed. One hundred years after Martin Luther posted his Ninety-five Theses on a church door in Germany and launched the Protestant Reformation, anti-Catholic sentiment was running high in England. However, the king acceded, permitting Charles to travel to Spain to broker a marriage deal. He sent trusted Buckingham to travel with Charles for this important 'diplomatic' mission.

In February of 1623 both Prince Charles and Duke Buckingham journeyed to Spain incognito, wearing false beards and wigs on their secret seventeenth-century covert operation. In Spain the newly unmasked pair was entertained by many parties at the royal court. Somehow, during this road trip, Buckingham and Charles emerged as best buddies. Such was the guile and cunning of Duke Buckingham.

The Spanish demanded that Charles repeal English anti-Catholic laws, an obvious impossibility in rabidly Protestant England. The mission was an abject failure. Upon their return, Charles and his new best mate Buckingham prevailed upon a reticent King James that it was time to declare war on Spain. The conflict ultimately lasted more than five years. Little was gained by either side except to add to the exceptional, mounting English war debt. It was an overwhelming fiasco.

By the time of James's death in March 1625, Charles and Buckingham had already assumed *de facto* domination of the realm. Never in the annals of English history has one man obtained such vast influence over two consecutive sovereigns.

Not everyone in the realm, however, was so enthralled with Buckingham, who was assassinated in 1628. King Charles refused to leave his chambers for two days, crying and grieving. In contrast, the public rejoiced, emphasizing the continual disconnect between the royal house and the people.

The end for Charles came in 1649, when he was beheaded for treason with a single ax blow by an anonymous executioner during the English Civil War.

Bacon, possessing an unbounded mind and knowledge, a man of science, died most appropriately. On a cold, snowy day in April 1626, Bacon pondered whether food could be preserved by freezing. His curiosity was piqued. Naturally, it was time to conduct more empirical scientific experiments. He bought a chicken and surrounded it with snow and ice, the first documented frozen chicken in history. But the experiment was never completed. A shivering Bacon's prolonged exposure to the wintry elements led to a serious, unfortunate case of pneumonia. Soon thereafter, our great scholar, philosopher, scientist, public servant and lawyer died.

The *Case of Sutton's Hospital* continued to be cited in United States cases into the 1990s.

Through the passage of time and the tumultuous ages, Sutton's Hospital, the institution, managed to survive. The almshouse still functions, helping the poor and disenfranchised on the original site purchased in 1611. However, the original buildings were mostly destroyed in Nazi bombing raids during World War II. The hospital has moved to another site, where it remains a valued part of the British National Institute of Health.

Thomas Sutton's vision continues to this day. His benevolent dream of caring for the less fortunate lives on with little realization of the considerable impact it would have on modern class actions.

All hail Thomas Sutton!

Chapter 5

1676: *Brown v. Vermuden*—Binding Absent Parties

It is dangerous for men in power if no one dares to tell them when they go wrong.
—St. Thomas Becket, stated personally to Herbert of Bosham, Life of St. Thomas Becket, *c. 1184*

Sleepy Derbyshire County, England, with its quiet, grassy pastures dotted with cattle and sheep, was an odd beneficiary of a cataclysmic event involving the king, the pope, an archbishop, and the king's trusted royal knights. The shockwaves reverberated across Western Europe, setting off a series of events that laid much of the groundwork for the law regarding binding absent parties in group representation lawsuits.

In about AD 43 the Romans conquered the area and promptly commenced mining iron and lead ore. Derbyshire first appears in the English historical record in 1048. An earthquake and wildfire were noted as causing great distress in the area. Robin Hood patrolled these woods about the time that Martin was suing the Nuthampstead parishioners. Remember the infamous sheriff of Nottingham?

Derbyshire remained the primary source of European lead ore during the Middle Ages, triggered by events throughout King Henry's reign from 1152 to 1189, and involving his most trusted confidant, Thomas Becket. Becket first met King Henry II in 1154 while working for the archbishop of Canterbury. One year later, he was already chancellor. As I mentioned in chapter 1, Becket was credited with creating the English national court system, an important historical milestone in the creation of equity law. Henry and Becket were good friends and enjoyed an excellent working relationship.

In 1162 Henry nominated Becket to be archbishop of Canterbury. The king sought a friendly, cooperative loyalist in Becket to institute church reforms. Upon Henry's nomination, Becket was elected to the post by a royal council of noblemen and bishops. But once he assumed the archbishop role, Becket deemed that his primary allegiance was to the pope and only secondarily to the Crown, much to Henry's disappointment and dismay.

King Henry sought clerical agreement to lessen his connection with Rome. Like King James's confrontation with Lord Edward Coke and his judges, Henry obtained agreement for his reforms from the higher English clergy—all except for Becket. Ongoing confrontations followed. Becket confiscated land owned by nobles for the church. He also excommunicated some of Henry's supporters for seeking to reduce the church's power.

In 1164 Henry tried Becket for contempt of royal authority and other issues while he was chancellor. Becket was convicted of the charge and fled to France, accepting King Louis VII's offer of protection.

In 1167 Pope Alexander III sent arbitrators/mediators to resolve the issues to end Becket's exile and facilitate his return to England.

King Henry proposed a compromise settlement that permitted Becket to return unmolested in 1170. Soon after his return, Becket excommunicated three royal loyalists.

In Henry's view, little had changed. "Will no one rid me of this turbulent priest?"[14] is the popular version of King Henry's inquiry, expressing frustration upon hearing about his former, most trusted confidant's continued defiant actions. Four loyal knights heard Henry's words and interpreted them as a generalized command to act. The knights rode off to Canterbury. Their intent: to escort Becket back to the king to account for his recent actions.

Upon arriving in Canterbury, true to their objective, the knights left their weapons outside the cathedral. But Becket refused to ride back with the knights to meet with Henry. Becket headed to the sacred chapel for prayer and protection. No harm or foul act would occur at the altar of the high sanctuary, would it?

Monks started bolting the doors, but Becket ordered that the doors be flung open. "A house of prayer shall not become a fortress!" he exclaimed.[15]

As the re-armed knights came rushing in, Becket realized that he was not safe either inside or outside the church. He still refused escort to the king. Finally, in a tense standoff, the knights, considering Becket a traitor, mercilessly hacked the archbishop to death right at the holy altar!

Immediate and intense repercussions rippled across Western Europe. Pope Alexander III promptly excommunicated King Henry. Seeking immediate penance, the king swore to go on crusade to the Holy Land and began an enormous church-building program throughout England. The church-building promise would require massive amounts of lead and iron ore for the structures, particularly to hold up the elaborate roofs and ceilings, water pipes, stained glass windows, and other forms of structural support.

The murder of Archbishop Thomas Becket, twelfth-century depiction.

Derbyshire and its iron and lead ore deposits were of keen interest to the contrition-filled king. Becket's murder launched the Derbyshire mining industry anew and created our future group representation defendants of *Brown v. Vermuden*—with the miners as legal adversaries of the church that sought discounted ore pricing to satisfy the former's tithe payment requirements. The area's mining remained in high gear for eight hundred years, all ignited by Henry's promise to the pope due to Becket's murder. Indeed, Becket's standing was so high that his canonization as Saint Thomas was completed a mere three years after the brutal slaying.

Fast forward five hundred years. The historical period leading to *Brown* was a time of great social and economic unrest in England. From 1642 to 1651, the English Civil War raged on, culminating in King Charles's execution in 1649. Non-monarch Oliver Cromwell ruled England for the next ten years or so until the monarchy was restored in 1660. Charles's brother, James II, a Roman Catholic, was crowned king, firing up existing religious discord that began with the Protestant Reformation and persisted for 150 years.

During the years 1665–1666, the Great Plague ravaged London, killing up to 20 percent of the city's population, with some estimates at two hundred thousand or more deaths. More Englishmen and women died from the Plague during this period than in either World War. London was not exclusively impacted. The Plague also found Derbyshire, spread there by fleas on rats.

In 1665 a box of fabric was delivered to a small village in Derbyshire named Eyam, bringing with it an infestation of Plague-carrying fleas. Eighty percent of the villagers in Eyam ultimately died as a result. This could have led to a terrible outbreak throughout Derbyshire if not for Eyam's brave rector, William Mompesson. He told the villagers: "Do not flee. That will only spread the infection to others. Stay here until the Plague runs its course."[16] He instituted a program requiring all coins used in business transactions to be dropped in vinegar as a disinfectant to sterilize the currency of commerce in and out of Eyam.

As a result, the Plague didn't spread to neighboring towns. Sadly, however, Mompesson's wife fell victim to the dreaded disease.

The following year, in September 1666, following ten months of drought, the Great Fire of London left a hundred thousand people homeless and destroyed London's city center. Overwhelming interruptions in both government and economic administration ensued.

Hence, a combination of revolution, religious and political upheaval, plagues, and fires all dislocated the standard flow of commerce. These brought labor shortages, helping the economic condition of serfs and upsetting government tax collection and payment of tithes to churches. Such was the setting that created the circumstances for *Brown v. Vermuden*.

With all the disorder and upheaval, the Derbyshire Roman Catholic Church's vicar found the parish's finances in desperate straits and determined that local miners were not paying their tithes to the church. The tithe required selling 10 percent of their output at below market rate prices mandated by the church. The vicar sued all miners of the parish in the Ecclesiastical Court to establish his 'customary rights' to the tithes from all parish mining operations. It was essentially a production tax on the miners to support the church. The defendant miners responded by naming four members to defend the suit in their place as group representatives of all the defendants.

The vicar won and the miners lost.

Sometime later Plaintiff Brown, the next vicar, sought to enforce the growing tithe debt against miner Vermuden in Chancery Courts. He based his claim upon liability established in the previous vicar's prevailing ecclesiastical lawsuit. Vermuden raised a reasonable defense. He was not a party to the earlier action, so how could he be bound by a prior judgment? Sounds like they needed a class action administrator back then to provide notice. He further argued the inequity of denial of appeal rights to the original judgment because he was not a party to that case. He had no chance to opt out.

On the latter point, the chancellor agreed! Yes, in equity, Vermuden should have a right to appeal, which he was denied in the first case, "because he is grieved by the Decree." He would have had the right to appeal if he had been designated as a party in the first case. So, go ahead and appeal. However, on appeal, the court held that Vermuden was in fact obligated to pay the tithe based upon the earlier decree, stating future suits "would be infinite, and impossible to be ended."

Now . . . feel the magic of equity.

The court found that the church's set purchase price was "too little" and ordered "a Commission to settle some more reasonable Recompense to the Miners." The chancellor recognized the church's right to buy 10 percent of the ore. But, at the same time, he threw open the issue of a fair price for these required sales. Vermuden most certainly had a greater interest in receiving a fair price for his ore than concern for who bought it from him, particularly if he could get the church off his back.

From the perspective of legal history, the significance of *Brown v. Vermuden* was English Chancery's earliest reported case explicitly holding that the judgment in a group representation setting was legal and binding on absent class members. In the second half of this book, we will see that this issue was not so easily settled in America.

Brown v. Vermuden didn't fade into the dustbin of history. The case was cited centuries later by the U.S. Supreme Court in *Hansberry v. Lee* (1940), a racially restrictive covenant due process violation action involving issues of notice and *res judicata*. We will examine this case in chapter 13, "1940–1950: Due Process Trumps Racially Restrictive Covenants."

The case was also cited by the Southern District of Ohio federal court, in *In Re Telectronic Pacing Systems* in 2001, concerning a proposed settlement in a nationwide class action regarding defective pacemakers, and cited in 2019 by the Eighth Circuit Court of Appeals in *Rogers v. Bryant*, where beggars claimed Arkansas' anti-loitering law violated their First Amendment free speech rights.

Returning to Mother England: For hundreds of years after Archbishop Becket's murder, the tomb of the later-anointed St. Thomas was an important, well-visited pilgrimage site, only eclipsed by Rome and Santiago de la Compostella in Galicia, part of modern-day Spain.

In 1538, three centuries after Archbishop Becket's murder, during the English Reformation and predating *Brown v. Vermuden*, King Henry VIII was determined to destroy the cult of St. Thomas. He issued an "Unsainting Proclamation," ordering Becket's shrine to be demolished, razed, and his remains burned. The veneration of a traitor to the king was condemned by the Protestant king as a heathen practice.

The treasures of the shrine totaling over £1 million were unceremoniously melted and added to the English treasury. These acts followed

Henry's annulment of his marriage to Catherine of Aragon and his subsequent marriage to Anne Boleyn without church approval, his declaration of himself as "Supreme Head of the Church of England," and his dissolution of monasteries. But sacrilege against the venerated saint was the last straw. A horrified pope finally excommunicated Henry VIII.

In 1688, during the Glorious Revolution, Protestants overthrew James II. But his life was spared; his head was not chopped off. This settled the issue of Protestant dominance in Britain once and for all.

Henry II broke his promise to the pope; he never went on crusade. But his dedication to church building is supported by a stunning discovery. In March 2020 scientists in the Swiss Alps conducted carbon dating tests of ice layers accumulated over the centuries. The ice layers revealed dramatic lead pollution increases emanating from Derbyshire soon after Becket's murder. Winds left the refuse from the smelting process in the distant mountains of Switzerland, proving Henry's rush to redeem his good standing with the pope.

Chapter 6

1762: A License to Wage War

Now and then we had a hope that if we lived and were good, God would permit us to be pirates.
  —Mark Twain, "Old Times on the Mississippi,"
  The Atlantic Monthly, *January 1875*

AUTHOR'S NOTE

In our research, we found numerous cases involving privateering, realizing that everyone from the sailor to the investor was a separate business enterprise. So I am going to have some fun and change the voice to a first-person narrative of a privateering entrepreneur in 1762 Bristol.

* * * * * * * * *

It's 1762. Bristol. Great Britain. I love the smell of salted sea air! I am feeling smashing. I stride with newly obtained Letters of Marque from Royal Admiralty in my pocket. In times of war, like now, these Letters ordain my ship's crew with license to pillage, destroy, even kill. Most importantly, to steal—at least for this voyage and others possessing the Letters.

We're proud privateers, seizing ships and goods from near and far away oceans. We even capture the crews as prisoners for future exchange with France, bringing them to the British Crown for payment. Legalized theft. Ah, the grand profits from our honorable privateering enterprise!

No, sir, we are not pirates. We are legal! Piracy has long been considered treasonous—punishable usually by death. But almost two hundred and fifty years ago, Parliament passed The Offence of the Sea Act of 1536. We are now businessmen. We take risks. But not as much as pirates, most of the time. When a war is raging, the King or the British Admiralty issue our Letters of Marque, Letters of Reprisal, or Official Commission Letters. Whatever you call 'em, it's all the same. With one of these documents, our actions are no longer treasonous. We're duly licensed to attack the enemy and their trading ships. We are deemed part of the Royal Navy, treated as enemy combatants, all within the law of nations. Beautiful, isn't it?!

If the captain and his crew are caught or captured, they avoid the gallows and are not slain like dogs—initially, at any rate. It is far better not to have your workforce executed en masse. They will not treat my men as criminal barbarians, but as prisoners of war.

Me, I am on the business side, queuing up investors, obtaining necessary documents, dealing with the greedy insurance companies, and purchasing supplies for a six-month journey at sea. Honestly, I have never sailed so far as to lose sight of land, except when I was a lad and got sick fishing. I admit to living vicariously from my crew's adventures and presence, and of course, the grand profits realized when they return.

Our home of Bristol boasts of John Cabot commencing his famed voyage to North America in 1497, almost two hundred years ago. The renowned and notorious pirate Blackbeard was born just by the port, close to where I grew up. Many pubs that I frequent, perhaps too often whilst joining my mates, boast of the Pirate Blackbeard supplying the local taverns with libations, and enjoying them there, as well. I sometimes wonder if he woke up to as many headaches after these outings as I do.

We in Bristol consider ourselves the second city of the Kingdom. In my limited years, I have seen the outskirts grow and greenbelts built upon. We are a city of enterprising merchants and tradesmen. Only London exceeds our trade, our prosperity, and all things that the outer world has to offer. We have many industries including textiles, copper and brass manufacturing, sugar production, a wide selection of grains, wine, olive oil, timber, rum, tobacco—the list goes on. Bristol is humming with economic activity. And joyfully, we have extremely limited nobility present, lacking the 'sophistication' of London.

Some say Liverpool is rising and surpassing us now. I have never visited. We are certainly the second most populated city in Britain, and I read that we are second in volume in shipping and commerce. Hard to think of Liverpool besting us.

Bristol is on the River Avon, six miles from the Bristol Channel and the sea. Ships are carried to the harbor on the river's tidal current, so captains must carefully time their entries into port. When the tidal current is low, the ships go aground and usually become stuck in the mud; they must wait for rising waters to depart. I hear wild talk about damming the river so that the port is always available. I do not see how this is possible.

I have heard that all maritime nations utilize privateer expeditions in war time. It's just too expensive for kings and queens to maintain standing navies. Consequently, they all use the existing merchant fleets for purposes of trade *and* war.

It does not cost the royals extra to issue the Letters of Marque. We must deposit a sizeable bond as surety for mint behavior. The Crown signs the piece of parchment, like the one I now hold, and awaits the returns. If a ship sinks or is unsuccessful, the Crown loses nothing.

Everyone knows our industry creates a staffing problem for the navy; as seamen, we earn a far better wage as privateers than as navy sailors. There I go again, living vicariously from the seamen's experiences.

Dear George III is our king and performing exceedingly well in this long war with France. We frequently hear of victories at sea. We are proud Englishmen right now. Those conquests motivate demand for our privateering efforts. How big is the demand? In 1761 the House of Commons reported 80,675 men were in the Royal Navy compared to 75,618 men on ships bearing Letters of Marque as privateers. No question we legal pirates, motivated by wealth, outperform those navy boys.

Whilst there is much pound sterling to be made, our license to wage war has limitations. We are only allowed to target ships that are adversaries of the King. On occasion, we are limited to specific sea lanes or locations. We, as privateers, are known to sometimes break these rules to bring in some extra pounds. Of course, *my* ships would never do that . . .

We privateers cannot take the ship, contents, or men as prizes for ourselves. No, we must bring the treasures back to the Admiralty Court to condemn and transfer to us. Then we distribute the booty via a pre-arranged contract.

The proceeds are divided by a percentage between sponsors, ship owners, captains, crew, and, of course, the sovereign. Ten percent to the Admiralty, five percent for customs duties, two-thirds of the remaining is apportioned to stockholders, and the final third, to the crew. Some crews receive no wages if under a "no booty, no pay" agreement. The crew is entitled to pillage the personal belongings of the enemy's crew or passengers. It's supposed to be equally shared but . . . ah well.

Whilst ye're out on the open seas, there is always opportunity for old-fashioned trading. In fact, our ships' primary purpose as we leave port is trade, but why not possess Letters of Marque as well? Ye never know what ye may stumble upon to make additional pounds.

The fighting is not always at sea, but sometimes we all end up in Admiralty or Chancery Court. Stockholders say that the company cheated 'em; the captain says that the company cheated him; the crew says that everyone cheated 'em. Usually, these various groups sue in unison, or on behalf of all the others with a similar interest. Someone should write a book about this concept sometime.

Due to the high costs involved, most voyages are organized as partnerships of four to six merchants, including the ship owner. So, I gather a group of investors to raise money and manage the voyage. Some ring me up as "the ship's husband." However, I do not want to take on the entire risk of a single expedition. I spread the possibility of failure across joint-stock systems. I have long-term mates who own the ships, both large and wee. Obviously, they have serious investments in ensuring that their ships return safely.

We merchant promoters do not usually travel with privateering ventures in person. Our lot always worry about losing bees and honey through pillage and embezzlement. My investors, holders of the stock of the enterprise, must trust me, and I must trust my captains and masters. My captain for this upcoming voyage is Kerry Ferrie, a mate from my teen years. He is a straight and narrow fellow, graduating from the Royal Naval Academy in Portsmouth. Kyle Windell is the ship's master, responsible for piloting the boat and running essential operations. He is your classic drinking buddy that I have known since childhood, always able to handle difficult tasks even after too many pints in the tavern.

In any business, trusted employees are essential. In the privateering business, having loyal agents on board is crucial for success.

Now that I hold these Letters of Marque, I need to obtain insurance coverage. One of my olde mates is an investor representing banks with superior contacts in the best insurance houses in London. Insurance rates have been amazingly stable even though the war has raged for years. About 7.5 percent of privateering ships are lost at sea, which, considering a standard spillage/spoilage rate of 3 or 4 percent on any voyage, is not too bad, except when you lose the whole ship, rather than just a portion of the cargo.

Some of my competitors do not carry insurance, but I admit discomfort in worrying about such losses. So far, I have been relatively lucky, losing only two ships in the last five years that this war has been raging.

We tend to follow British Navy predetermined food ration levels for each sailor. These rations include one pound of scones and a gallon of ale each day. It's important that the ale possesses quality ingredients. Nothin' worse than sailors unhappy with the quality of their ale rations. Each week, the sailors also receive four pounds of beef, two pounds of salted pork, three-eighths of a twenty-four-inch cod, two pints of peas, six ounces of butter, and between eight and twelve ounces of cheese.

Ale for these journeys usually had a 1–3 percent alcohol content, and most sailors didn't drink their gallon each day but saved it up for non-shift periods.

Kerry Ferrie, my naval academy graduate mate, always provides a list of necessary armaments, cannon, firearms, powder, and shot for his voyages. I must certify these purchases for the insurance coverage.

As for masts, sails, and ropes, Kyle Windell, the ship's master, insists on personally examining and purchasing these critical items. Obviously, if these replacements are found defective at sea, the entire crew could be doomed.

* * *

Alas, I must now take leave of my fantasy of managing an eighteenth-century privateering enterprise. Time to transition back to historical economics and group representation cases. It was a fun romp whilst it lasted.

* * *

The first quarter of the 1700s experienced a commercial revolution, the spoils spurred on by New World markets from the Age of Exploration. Along with this unprecedented, rampant economic growth came an explosive, newly created stock market. However, as during any period of rapid economic and stock market growth, stock fraud and mismanagement followed. Economically and legally, the crews of seaman were a voluntary entrepreneurial association for the purpose of joint profit and adventure. When disputes arose affecting people with similar interests, a natural outgrowth of that entrepreneurial association was group litigation. This was spurred on by the inherent difficulty of handling joint legal matters individually; enough reason to prosecute a legal controversy as a group when all are denied just compensation.

The English stock market crashed in 1718, an event referred to as the "South Sea Bubble." Investor lawsuits promptly followed. *Chancy v. May* (1722) is a notable case. The president and treasurer of a company, on behalf of themselves and "all other proprietors and partners," sued thirteen other officers and/or partners. They sought an accounting regarding a privateering enterprise, as embezzlement, misapplication of funds, and mismanagement was highly suspected. In the legal sense, an accounting is an audit overseen by the court to help ensure there is no cheating.

The defendants argued that the lawsuit was defective, as there were other "proprietors" who were also shareholders, and thus potential similar defendants. But the plaintiffs did not name them. If the case were to proceed, they argued, the named defendants could face a future multiplicity of similar suits from other plaintiffs while other shareholders would ride scot-free. It would be unfair. The Chancery Court thought otherwise.

An early, rather simple declaration, seemingly consistent with modern class action principles, stated:

> Because it was in behalf of themselves, and all other the proprietors of the same undertaking, except the defendants, and so all the rest were in effect parties. It would be impractical to make them all parties by name . . . no coming at justice if all were to be made parties.[17]

Translation: You cannot dismiss the present claims because others not before the court may also have similar claims. The present plaintiffs are standing in for the unnamed plaintiffs. In the modern world, we would call "the present plaintiffs" the "class action representatives."

From the organized chaos of warring privateers come the initial hints of an "adequacy of representation" concerns—does the group or class representatives adequately represent the absent members to address the difficult problem involving lots of parties at one time. This sounds like our modern-day class action, in which courts permit a final settlement, and class action administrators cannot obtain more than a 25 percent claims response rate from class members. Group litigation is inherently imperfect.

The Chancey plaintiffs were permitted to proceed without both the necessary parties (the other partner defendants) or the actual consent of the similarly situated non-parties (the other plaintiffs). An imperfect situation, but let's proceed anyway.

However, seamen were not always so fortunate.

In the 1751 case of *Leigh v. Thomas*, two seamen sought an accounting regarding prize money. These two, seemingly leaders among the crew, held a written power of attorney on behalf of sixty-four members out of a total crew of eighty. They possessed no express authority to represent the balance of the crew. The ship's articles provided for the appointment of agents but lacked any specificity to institute a lawsuit.

These representative agents made things more complicated by claiming additional shares of prize money for acting as agents for the others. This argument is similar to present-day class action representatives receiving a representation fee, sometimes called an "incentive award." However, the articles didn't mention these additional shares or any other representation award.

The defendants argued that the lawsuit could not proceed without the entire crew being a party. The court agreed to dismiss the lawsuit. In this case, the concern was that the remaining sixteen crew members might later assert that they never authorized representation or subtraction for a "representation share." The court nullified the agreement. The sixty-four crew members did not hold the same interest as the other sixteen. The defendants, the court rationalized, must be protected from multiple lawsuits—a result inconsistent with *Chancey*.

Fast forward to the Napoleonic Wars. In 1806 the captain of a privateer voyage sued the ship's owners for an accounting of the captured booty. Initially, Captain Good did not file a lawsuit for everyone, but the court instructed him to do so. He complied, and the case proceeded. In the early 1800s case of *Good v. Blewitt*, Lord

Chancellor John Scott, earl of Eldon, held that requiring joinder of all necessary parties would be excused because many potential plaintiffs, some geographically dispersed, others deceased or unknown, could be "dispensed with."[18] Translation: We will not worry about all the potential claimants. Everyone bound by the judgment are defendants before the court. If other plaintiffs come forward in the future, we will deal with those issues then. This was the opposite result of *Leigh v. Thomas*.

The decision in *Good v. Blewitt* sounds like equity to me, the twenty-first-century storyteller. We can see that crewmembers and investors met uncertainty when instituting legal proceedings seeking redress for their claims. It sounds no different from the uncertain legal environment that I encounter today when lawyers can never assure me of an outcome.

Besides the legal issues, privateering also raised public policy concerns. When war ended and peace ensued, our hardy seamen were reluctant to return to fishing, merchant ships, or other humbler trades on the ocean. Instead, they turned to piracy. They were experienced and courageous. Like anyone, they wanted to make more money using their existing job skills. Terminating privateers is the incubator for future troubles.

A modern-day example comes to mind: the United States arming tribesmen in the 1980s to drive Russian forces out of Afghanistan. After that success, these experienced fighters morphed into the Taliban, who are still causing us problems today.

War, in general, always generates more troubles down the line. Consider the war raging in the early 1760s discussed earlier. It left the British treasury with massive war debt. This, in turn, forced King George III and Parliament to tax the American colonies, triggering resentment and, ultimately, prompting the American Revolution.

However, privateers remained part of the political and economic reality of the seas. American colonists used privateers successfully against the British during the Revolutionary War. In fact, Article 1, Section 8, of the U.S. Constitution provides Congress the power to tax, declare war, and issue letters of marque and reprisal, although they haven't done so since President James Madison's request in 1815 to counter Algerian vessels during the Second Barbary War.

In the 1856 Declaration of Paris, all major European powers agreed to abolish privateering. The United States was not a signatory to this declaration but has followed the agreement's mandate anyway. During the Civil War, however, the Confederate states—at that time acting as a wholly separate nation from the United States—undertook several successful privateering ventures.

Bristol eventually solved the problem of low tides. In 1809 the "Floating Harbour" was finalized. A cutting-edge locking system traps water in the city's central harbor, allowing ships and boats to stay buoyant without being disturbed by changing tides. It is still in use today.

Now, I just need to figure out how to get back to Bristol, 1762. There is no great sailing ship to be found. Ah, those grand ol' days—to be a privateer again! I have always been an entrepreneurial sort, thirsty for adventure. Perhaps there is a way to go back with Letters of Marque in the pocket of my waistcoat. Once again, I would lift a pint and enjoy the life of a privateer well before the era of horseless carriages, airplanes, and microwaves. But instead, turn the page with me to hear a tale of American Revolutionary War hero William West, whose privateering activities shaped the first major group representation to be decided by a legendary U.S. Supreme Court justice.

Part II

The New World

From Revolution to Equality: Class Actions, American Style

Chapter 7

1820: General West and the Licentious Republic

It appears to me, that they were guided by the mob, whose intentions were to murder the pilot, and destroy the vessel. But I hope it will, by Your Lordship's representation, be the means of a change of government in this licentious republic.
—British Captain John Smith to the Lord Council,
July 12, 1764

In March 1761, Colonel William West bought a five-hundred-acre property in Scituate, Rhode Island, from future signer of the Declaration of Independence Stephen Hopkins, a past (and future) Rhode Island governor and chief justice of the colony. Many years after purchasing the West's property, "The Big House," the largest in Rhode Island, was finally completed.

After West's death, his son brought a lawsuit, *West v. Randall*, regarding his father's estate. The son sued individuals charged with settling his father's finances. He sued as a single heir-at-law, even

The Big House, Scituate, Rhode Island, photographed early 1900s.

though many other possible beneficiaries existed. The dispute would eventually be heard by the preeminent U.S. Supreme Court Justice and legal scholar Joseph Story, creating the first significant American class action jurisprudential benchmark.

Little has been written or documented about William West, the great-grandson of a Pilgrim, a Revolutionary War militia brigadier general, Rhode Island Supreme Court justice, and deputy governor of Rhode Island. Much of our knowledge originates from his great-grandson, George West, who spent twenty-five years accumulating information about the life of his patriotic forefather, resulting in a modest biography published in 1919. Only fifty copies of the book were printed. Part of George's investigation included a visit to The Big House sometime before publication, providing insight from that vantage point in history.

Before the Revolutionary War, William West was an extremely successful land dealer, farmer, and trader. West fought in the French and Indian War, the same worldwide dispute between the English and French discussed by our hardworking privateer in the previous chapter. Different theater, same war. (In Europe, the conflict is called the Seven Years' War.) George Washington was a British army colonel in that war. West was called *colonel* before the beginning of the Revolutionary War, but no evidence has been found indicating he was officially part of the British military.

The foundation of West's and all of Rhode Island's independent characters arose partly from King Charles II's (the son of beheaded Charles I) historic Royal Charter of 1663, which formed the new colony. The charter gave Rhode Islanders the right to practice the religion of their choosing, the first time a monarch ever made such a grant. Rhode Islanders were also granted the right to govern their own colony, similar to the grant King James bestowed on the Channel Islanders in 1204.

Because of its geographic setting, Rhode Island's commerce was dependent on maritime trade. It lacked a developed hinterland to obtain the necessary raw materials for the creation of manufacturing industries, but it did possess excellent natural harbors at Newport and Providence, providing a grand base for trading with other American colonies, and with Madeira, Suriname, and the West Indies.

By 1731 Rhode Island had established direct trade with Holland, the Mediterranean, and England. In 1740 a fleet of 120 vessels from Newport and Providence traded with foreign ports. By 1763 that number had expanded to over 530 ships from Newport alone.

William West's first recorded business venture was as an innkeeper in 1758, a few miles east of the later-acquired Big House property. He was known as a shrewd businessman, obtaining a substantial fortune as a land dealer. His farm had at least a hundred cows and many horses, oxen, and sheep. The farming operation was a major business. West was known to bring up to fifteen hundred pounds of cheese to Providence in a single trip. He was also an active trader in molasses, the key ingredient in rum production, which was fast becoming a staple of the fledgling New England economy.

Colonel West was extremely well-respected by his community. From 1760 to 1790 he was closely tied to the political and social life of Scituate and Rhode Island. He was a resident for a scant two years when first elected as a deputy to the colonial legislature, then he was re-elected to the post for twelve more terms. He was chosen as town moderator in 1765, and as justice of the peace from 1774 to 1776. He never received a salary to perform any of these civic duties; he was a dedicated and trusted public servant.

Possessing great wealth and an outgoing personality, West spared no expense when building The Big House. The home contained the highest style of colonial architecture. A front door framed with everlasting oak, as seen in the pictures taken by his great-grandson, exemplified the high standards of detail and workmanship throughout the home. The home had many large rooms, including a famed, massive, high-ceilinged attic described as large enough to serve as a public meeting hall.

The house was built over a well. The wine cellar was cleverly designed to submerge wine in the cool well water. Of course, the home had a large parlor for entertaining and holding meetings. A wealthy businessman and politician, the largest house, and an outgoing personality all led to extravagant, lavish entertaining among the free-spirited Rhode Islanders—an ideal environment for political and business networking and strategizing.

Additionally, Rebels were routinely quartered at The Big House. West unsparingly provided maximum effort to the revolutionary cause of independence from Britain.

Concurrent with the July 4, 1876, Scituate Centennial Independence Day celebrations, at the request of town authorities, Mr. C. C. Beaman delivered *An Historical Sketch of The Town of Scituate, R.I.* Beaman recounted talking with a Mr. Welcome Arnold,

The Big House, North Scituate, Rhode Island, built in the 1760s.

who had died twenty years earlier. Arnold was present when The Big House was completed and was a guest at many of West's gatherings. Arnold reported that the rum flowed freely, but the wine was served most sparingly, obviously based on availability (or maybe too many guests).

In 1765 the British Parliament passed a series of laws known collectively as the Townshend Acts. They were five different statutes named after the chancellor of the exchequer, akin to America's secretary of the treasury. The Acts placed taxes on many important imported goods, including glass, paint, lead, and tea. American port cities expressed their ire by refusing to accept these goods. Rhode Islanders were more vigorous in their opposition than most colonies, based both on their dependence on foreign trade and their possession of the unique charter granted by King Charles II in 1663 permitting self-governance. Further shades of the Channel Islanders' struggle over five hundred years prior.

In 1766 Parliament passed the Stamp Act, a tax on many printed materials, legal documents, newspapers, magazines, even playing cards. The tax had to be paid with British currency, not colonial paper money. Further shades of Sir Otes and the Channel Islanders. The British needed tax revenue to continue financing the French and Indian War. However, the colonists had never felt threatened by the French. It was a major political mistake to anger colonial newspaper and magazine editors who had the power of the print to mold the pulse of the populace. The British did not appreciate that the pen was mightier than the sword. Cries of "No Taxation Without Representation" began their historic refrain.

Rhode Islanders ignored the Stamp Act's enforcement. The colonial governor, Samuel Ward, refused to take the required oath for executing the Stamp Act, explaining to London that doing so would bring swift, inevitable ruin to the local government. Riots in Newport and attacks on the homes of the stamp distributors followed. Rhode Islanders were so universally opposed that a British captain's report to the Lord Council in London called the colony "the licentious republic." They completely disregarded all accepted rules or conventions. Rhode Islanders proudly wore the "licentious" moniker.

Because of Rhode Island's dependence on the sea and trade, along with Great Britain's taxation and importation policies, smuggling and tax evasion became the norm. Rhode Island judges, in almost open defiance of the king, would delay tax and smuggling cases for years, making effective enforcement almost impossible. Rhode Islanders had a common determination to continue their independent ways.

The Boston Massacre of 1770 resulted in only five people being killed. However, the colonists had never before been shot down by British troopers. Rhode Islanders continued refining their smuggling and tax evading strategies over the ensuing years.

British customs commissioners sought more forceful actions to prevent smuggling and tax evasion. In March 1772 the *Gaspee*, a

British Navy armed schooner, was dispatched to Narragansett Bay. The lieutenant in charge was particularly aggressive, stopping every boat it encountered, insisting upon the strictest enforcement of the trade acts. Then the *Gaspee* confiscated a boatload of undeclared rum. Its captain was sent to Boston for trial. Rhode Islanders were aghast. This was a direct violation of the Rhode Island Royal Charter of 1663, which decreed that arrests in the colony must be tried in the colony.

On June 10, 1772, the *Gaspee* ran aground in shallow water while chasing a smuggling ship south of Providence. Word quickly spread that this dastardly vessel was stuck, waiting for high tide to set it free. The licentious Rhode Islanders moved quickly, setting the *Gaspee* ablaze, leaving it destroyed, while also wounding the hated, overzealous lieutenant. It was the first colonial attack on the British military—years before Lexington and Concord.

King George ordered a commission of inquiry to investigate the *Gaspee* affair. But the licentious Rhode Islanders refused to cooperate. They would provide no aid to any force that dared to threaten their liberties. Creation of the commission gave rise to the Committees of Correspondence: The colonists set up a communication network to discuss their relationship with Britain. You might call it a Revolutionary War–era version of an email or Facebook group. Many colonial assemblies passed resolutions moving future Americans closer to revolution.

In 1773 Parliament passed the Tea Act, granting the East India Company exclusive rights to sell tea in the colonies. The Boston Tea Party resulted—one of the most historical, renowned, political protests in history. The first meeting of the Continental Congress was held, with Rhode Island sending its two most distinguished citizens, Samuel Ward, the governor who refused to enforce the Stamp Act, and former governor Stephen Hopkins, the seller of the land where William West constructed The Big House. In September

Sons of Liberty marker commemorating the Gaspee Affair, Providence, Rhode Island, 1772.

1774 West was appointed to serve on the Committee of Correspondence for Scituate.

In 1775 the governor appointed Colonel West as second in command to defend the shores of Narragansett Bay. West gave his time and money to the revolutionary cause, but his profitable farm and other business enterprises were neglected. In a town meeting held on April 28, 1777, West was appointed to raise soldiers. Such was the trust and confidence that Scituate placed in our hero, William West.

Rhode Island enjoyed the finest harbor in North America. In the early days of the uprising, the British considered it the seat of the rebellion. Indeed, Rhode Islanders deemed themselves *the* revolutionary vanguard. Their unusual charter afforded them the greatest degree of independent, local government. If defeated, they had the most to lose. The British quickly created a major blockade at Newport to prevent privateers from exiting the harbor and menacing British merchant shipping. Colonials had no navy to speak of, so they depended on privateers to provide defense at sea. In 1778 now Brigadier General West led the Rhode Island Militia in an attempted siege of British-controlled Newport. But new Royal Navy ships arrived, repulsing the siege. This was the only Revolutionary War battle in licentious Rhode Island.

At the time, it was said that the colonists were "privateering mad," joining these nautical ranks with "excessive rage" and draining colonial army ranks as it did for the British Navy during the Seven Years' War. Privateer pay was better than the pay in the fighting infantry. Governor Hopkins was credited with persistently lobbying the Continental Congress to expedite payments into the pockets of continental seamen. The maritime court had already acquired a notorious reputation for summary condemnation of British property. No record of any 'group representation' lawsuits in America regarding these endeavors can be found. The early patriots were apparently able to work out these matters efficiently without the necessity of court action.

How popular was privateering? Rhode Island Governor Nicholas Cooke's original supply of forty-seven printed Continental Commissions or Letters of Marque and Reprisal were issued within six months. He was forced to sign twelve handwritten commissions before more could even be printed. Successful privateering provoked rage, performing a crucial role in the American Revolution. There were an estimated seven hundred commissioned ships compared to roughly one hundred U.S. Navy ships. George Washington and Thomas Paine owned stock in privateers. Indeed, privateers saved Washington's army near Boston at the beginning of the war, obtaining a large shipment of British armaments.

Benjamin Franklin exerted great effort to commission privateers while he was stationed in Paris. He sought to secure the release of

American soldiers detained in British prisons through a prisoner exchange. However, the American military apprehended few British fighters. Hence, he sought privateers to capture British sailors to obtain an inventory of prisoners for bartering purposes.

William West heavily financed two privateering ventures. The ships were lost at sea, along with West's significant investment. Before the war, West had been a successful farmer. The war effort diverted his attention, and the depreciation of continental currency's value caused him financial ruin, a precursor of events leading to the *West v. Randall* lawsuit. Other great patriots of that time met the same fate.

In October 1779 the British left the colony. At least in Rhode Island, the urgent justification for armed privateers disappeared.

In 1787 the Constitutional Convention was held in Philadelphia. Ever the licentious republic, Rhode Island refused to even send representatives. William West, an active anti-Federalist, was extremely opposed to the Constitution. For instance, on July 4, 1788, Providence residents held an ox roast celebrating independence and the newly created Constitution. Among the scheduled festivities was a formal reading of this lofty document. In outrage, West, while holding the post of superior court judge, led almost one thousand armed men to protest the event. Civil unrest was narrowly averted when the Federalists agreed to celebrate only independence, not the Constitution's adoption. Licentious indeed. Hopefully, there was enough roasted ox for everyone.

In 1790 Rhode Island was the last colony to support ratification of the U.S. Constitution. Quite rambunctious, as well.

In 1791 West made judicial history, but not the type anyone desires. He sought to use continental currency to pay the mortgage on his farm. In the very first U.S. Supreme Court decision, *West v. Barnes*, the court found that he didn't properly satisfy court filing requirements mandated by statute. Hence, he lost the chance to obtain a judicial determination regarding the legal basis of his currency and, thereby, save his long-cherished homestead. In 1792, due to West's severely declining financial circumstances, he was forced to enter a complicated financial transaction to satisfy creditors.

His finances found him in debtor's prison. In 1814 William West died at the age of eighty-three in relative poverty and obscurity, buried across the road from The Big House. His grave was marked by a single rough field stone—not even a tombstone. No painting, drawing, or likeness of this contributing founder of our nation exists.

After West's death, his son, also named William, brought the lawsuit, *West v. Randall*, regarding his father's estate. The son sued people responsible for settling the colonel's finances. He sued as a single heir-at-law when many other possible beneficiaries existed.

West v. Randall was decided in 1820 by the legendary U.S. Supreme Court Justice Joseph Story. Story was faced with the following factual contentions: While our hero accumulated many debts, he also held significant assets. Demonstrating his core decency, West desired satisfying creditors and leaving his family with a clear remainder of the leftover estate, liberated from financial troubles.

His advancing age left him unable to negotiate and effectively handle all the necessary transactions. He entered into an agreement with Job Randall, Jeremiah Phillips, and two others, deceased by the time of the lawsuit, who had the authority to settle those affairs. Randall, Phillips, and the others had adequate liquid funds to effectuate the transactions. West conveyed The Big House property to Randall, Phillips, and the others in trust. They in turn provided West with $3,500 in lawful silver money and a bond of defeasance. This meant that once all the transactions were completed and the creditors paid with a resulting clear residue, The Big House trust conveyance would be voided. The Big House was designated as security to protect Randall and Phillips. Once Randall and Phillips paid off West's debts, they would return the property to him.

William West was never able to pay them back.

So, in the underlying Rhode Island state court case, West's son was one heir of many, but he was the only named plaintiff in the lawsuit. He sought an accounting, claiming that Randall took the family farm in his own name. The son claimed that documents signed by his father, transferring the bond of defeasance to Randall, were fraudulent. It had no witnesses or seal. It was not even recorded until many years later. The son also claimed that while his father lay on his deathbed, Randall promised to deliver the estate to West's heirs. Randall refuted those accusations, arguing that the transfer was organized years earlier, he had settled all the colonel's debts, and the value of the farm was fair compensation for all his time, effort, and expense.

Randall denied even being a trustee and claimed that his only obligation arose from the bond of defeasance. Randall additionally raised defenses that the claims were also barred by statute of limitations and statute of frauds. Both defendants raised objections to the failure of the son to join the other heirs at law of William West. The record was factually barren regarding why they were omitted, much to the frustration of Justice Story. The challenge regarding this omission gave rise to Story's decision, setting the first significant class action precedent in America.

Justice Story was among the most preeminent legal scholars and jurists in American history. His role in the early definition of U.S. equity law, and by extension class actions, is so great that the next chapter is devoted to his life and writings. While *West v. Randall* is generally considered a mere footnote to Story's scholarship and legal impact, it's the starting point of class action jurisprudence in America. Such is the standing of great men and women.

In this case, Justice Story acted much like the English judges in eyre. From the beginning of the American nation until after the Civil War, Supreme Court justices "rode the circuit." The term springs from individual justices also acting as traveling appeal court judges, riding from courthouses to public meeting rooms within their assigned territories, setting up court in designated places whenever a controversy required further adjudication. For many judges during this period, judicial service required lots of travel. Congress, at the time, wanted justices to interact with the citizenry, and it saved money from hiring an entire phalanx of appeal court judges. Hence, while *West v. Randall* is a preeminent case of a Supreme Court justice and reported in the *Supreme Court Reporter*, it's more akin to a federal appeals court decision. These were the wild days of the early American judicial system, still in its formative stages.

Justice Story was faced with the existing Necessary Parties Rule, requiring any person with a particular interest in the proceeding to be joined as a party. During this stage of American jurisprudence, judges routinely relied on English precedent, but it wasn't binding. Justice Story's *West* decision summarized his understanding of the current state of the law regarding numerous parties, a multiplicity of lawsuits, the need for judicial efficiency, and ensuring that injustice did not occur. He wrote,

> It is a general rule in equity, that all persons materially interested, either as plaintiffs or defendants in the subject matter of the bill ought to be made parties to the suit, however numerous they may be. The reason is that the court may be enabled to make a complete decree between the parties, may prevent future litigation by taking away the necessity of a multiplicity of suits, and may make it perfectly certain, that no injustice shall be done, either to the parties before the court, or to others, who are interested by a decree, that may be grounded upon a partial view only of the real merits.
>
> [F]or where the parties are very numerous, and the court perceives, that it will be almost impossible to bring them all before the court; or where the question is of general interest, and a few may sue for the benefit of the whole; or where the parties form a part of a voluntary association for public or private purposes, and may be

fairly supposed to represent the rights and interests of the whole; in these and analogous cases, if the bill purports to be not merely in behalf of the plaintiffs, but of all others interested, the plea of the want of parties will be repelled, and the court will proceed to a decree. Yet, in these cases, so solicitous is the court to attain substantial justice, that it will permit the other parties to come in under the decree, and take the benefit of it, or to shew it to be erroneous, and award a re-hearing; or will entertain a bill or petition, which shall bring the rights of such parties more distinctly before the court, if there be certainty or danger of injury or injustice.[19]

In this case, Justice Story found, "[n]o reason is shown on the face of the bill, why the other heirs, having the same common interest, are not parties to it. The answer gives their names, and shows them within the jurisdiction of the court, and as defendants, they might have been joined in this suit without touching the jurisdiction of the court, for they are all resident in this state."[20] Additionally, a personal representative of the deceased William West was not a designated party, another basis for Justice Story to deny the appeal.

Story was none too compelled by West's other factual contentions either. Why didn't West's attorneys join the other known heirs, all residing in Rhode Island? The reason is unknown. But from the perspective of cases with numerous necessary parties, it was among the defects causing the case to be lost.

The legal world did not treat the Wests kindly.

C. C. Beaman, the writer of the 1876 Scituate centennial address, was disturbed when he visited The Big House. It didn't have even a placard to "leave us a memorial of their day, in this edifice and may it stand a century longer."[21] Photographs of the Big House in great-grandson George's book were taken between 1900 and 1905. Mr. Beaman's dream that the edifice would stand at least another century was not to be realized. Our hero's memory takes another hit.

A 1980 report of the Rhode Island Historical Preservation Commission regarding Scituate contains no mention of The Big House, obviously long gone. Local tax records show that a residence was built quite close to The Big House site in 1929. With the location of this 'new' construction, close to where The Big House once stood, one must conclude that the latter was already demolished.

James N. Arnold spent more than thirty-five years collecting and publishing historical Rhode Island records. He was told in September 1904, "Gov. William West was buried next to the parents of Stephen Hopkins, on the West farm in meadow and nearly opposite of the house across the road."[22] At that time, simple fieldstones marked each grave. A photograph of the fieldstone, taken by great-grandson George West, is in the box below.

In the mid-twentieth century, a tombstone was provided by the National Cemetery Service of the Department of Veterans Affairs, obtained by an unknown patriot, bearing the inscription "Co. Wm.

Burial ground with fieldstone markers, Scituate, Rhode Island, 1900s.

Grave of Brigadier General William West, Revolutionary War veteran, Providence, Rhode Island, 1733–1816.

West R.I Mil Rev. War." Later that tombstone was replaced with a newer, updated one, also provided by the federal government bearing the inscription "William West Brig Gen 3D Providence County Regt

Rev War 1733–1816." Many mature trees have now grown where George West and James Arnold only saw meadow.

The cemetery does not receive perpetual care. A few Rhode Island Historical Cemetery Commission volunteers try to maintain the large number of small, ancient cemeteries, usually lying in sparsely wooded areas. Sometimes this civic chore is performed by the Boy or Girl Scouts.

Today the most notable event recounted in this story is Gaspee Days, celebrated each year in Pawtuxet Village commemorating the *Gaspee* affair. A parade, festival, Revolutionary War battle reenactment, burning of the *Gaspee* in effigy, arts and crafts displays, and races all comprise the commemoration of the brave revolutionary fighters who helped build our nation.

Most importantly to all Americans, let's give a huge thank you, along with a rousing cheer and a moment of respectful silence, for William West, a patriot of the highest order. Though he died in relative poverty, West's life must long be remembered for his generous self-sacrifice to Scituate and to our fledging nation.

Chapter 8

1820–1845: Joseph Story Teaching America Equity

He was teacher to a Nation. And he was always teaching. As a member of the United States Supreme Court, he handed down opinions that were, on matters of general interest, often lectures on the duties of good citizenship directed to the literate public.

—*Calvin Woodard*[23]

The second U.S. Supreme Court chief justice, John Marshall, would strike like lightning. In his speedy rulings, the chief would proclaim, "Defendant wins. Mr. Justice Story will give the reasons why."[24] Appointed by President John Adams, Marshall's unique and fabled decision-making process became legendary during the deliberation of difficult cases. Marshall was supremely confident of Joseph Story's legal abilities. Story crafted beautifully written and well-reasoned opinions, accompanied with generous citations to existing law and precedent.

Joseph Story, son of a Boston Tea Party participant, was an American legal giant. He was perhaps equaled, but not surpassed, by other great luminary minds, including John Marshall, Louis Brandeis, Oliver Wendell Holmes, Jr., and William O. Douglas. A prolific author of Supreme Court opinions, while on the bench he also wrote eleven legal treatises regarding equity jurisprudence and procedure, constitutional law, conflict of laws, agency, partnerships, bailments, promissory notes, pleadings, and bills of exchange, while also holding the first endowed professorship at Harvard Law School.

Beyond inspiring as to how much someone can accomplish in a single lifetime, Story's legacy overwhelms in its breadth.

For our class action history stories, his *Commentaries on Equity Jurisprudence* provided American judges and lawyers significant building blocks of legal thought that enabled the growth of this area of law from medieval group litigation to modern class actions.

In the first chapter, I told the story of equity's creation and administration in England. But the American social experience was different. The initial settlement of America was rural in character, a much simpler life than in England with its large cities and towns, manufacturing enterprises, and overseas wars. Colonial lawyers were almost nonexistent. The colonies' judicial systems fit those more limited needs, and not more. The technicalities of wills and mortgages were not an issue. Just travel a little farther west and get some land. There was no need to fight over issues of wealth and money like in the mother country.

The "Conscience of the King," the source of equity in England, was irrelevant in our new country. Any judicial power emanating from a nonattributable source was deemed abhorrent. Indeed, most political grievances were against the Crown for its arbitrary nature. No prior ecclesiastical court tradition existed here either. The importance and pride of trial by jury of one's peers had taken root in Colonial America. The colonists resisted equity concepts for fear of losing this essential right. Puritans just assumed that the courts would always be inherently equitable.

In colonial courts, corrective rules—the essence of equity—were unnecessary. Rather, these tribunals found ways to instill equity into their decision making. In contrast, equity courts were completely absent in New England. New York, Maryland, and South Carolina had operated chancery courts continuously for long periods of time, accommodating a fair amount of litigation. New York and South Carolina were under the direct control of the king, called *provincial colonies*, while Maryland was a *proprietary colony*, owned by a person or family. Charter colonies such as Rhode Island, that we saw in the previous chapter, were prevalent in New England.

In the end, the U.S. Constitution extended federal judiciary power to "cases in law and equity" but provided no hint of equity's meaning or scope. The clause was inserted with some dispute, as many were concerned that the Constitution did not provide the right for juries in civil trials. In response, Alexander Hamilton's Federalist 83 (there were eighty-five, so, near the end) stated that the "separation of the equity from the legal jurisdiction is peculiar to the English system of jurisprudence," but "great advantages result from the separation."[25] So rumblings regarding equity's inclusion in the Constitution existed.

It was not a blank canvas, but no clear rule book existed instructing how to set up judicial procedures for our new country. With a fresh start, the early days of the American Republic's equity rulings were created by judges. No statutory basis existed. This was prime ground for eminent judicial scholar Joseph Story to pontificate and mold our nation's legal thinking.

In 1805, when Story was twenty-five years old, he was elected to the Massachusetts House of Representatives. In 1807 he chaired a committee to draft a bill for the creation of an equity court, but that was ultimately unsuccessful. In 1808 Story served a term in the U.S. Congress before quickly returning to the Massachusetts legislature in

1811. He was promptly elected Speaker of the House, but he didn't last long in that lofty office. In 1812 President James Madison nominated Story to the Supreme Court, making him the youngest person ever appointed to this illustrious post.

At only thirty-two years old, Story joined the U.S. Supreme Court for life.

In 1820, while on the Supreme Court, Story served as a delegate to the Massachusetts Constitutional Convention. As its chairman of the Commission on the Judiciary, he drafted a four-point proposal for judicial reform. He sought the creation of a separate state court for equity jurisdiction. Again, the measure failed. Story's persistence to create equity courts demonstrates the importance of equity law in an incredibly young, but mature, legal mind.

The previous chapter discussed Justice Story's opinion in *West v. Randall*. This case really only gains attention today from a special class of law nerds (like me) who are interested in class action judicial history. However, it provided a thorough review of English representative suits that discussed disposing of the standard objections of the lack of necessary parties and the exceptions.

In *West*, the necessary parties were known and available. However, Story's legal opinions and writings were so great and varied that the deluge of legal brilliance overwhelms the importance of our topic of discussion. *West v. Randall*, validating a wide swath of English common law about the necessity of sometimes instituting group representation procedures, is considered a preeminent milestone in the development of class action law in the United States if for no other reason than due to the dearth of substantive cases in the early American experience.

Justice Story is most famed for his opinions in *Martin v. Hunter's Lessee*, *The Amistad* case, and *Swift v. Tyson*. *Martin* is the landmark case asserting the Supreme Court's ultimate authority over state courts regarding the interpretation of federal civil law. Story's decision determined that federal power came from the people and not the states. Hence, based upon that rationale, the High Court could review state court decisions concerning federal law.

The Amistad, termed a "freedom suit" for slaves, was considered the most important slavery ruling prior to the *Dred Scott* decision (denying freed slaves' citizenship). In *The Amistad*, the Africans successfully argued that they were kidnapped in violation of all international law regarding human slave trade. Thus, their mutiny and subsequent sailing of the ship to America seeking asylum were lawful. Story, writing the opinion for the court on a case argued by former President John Quincy Adams, stated that "it was the ultimate right of all human beings in extreme cases to resist oppression, and to apply force against ruinous injustice."[26] Africans had a right to resist "unlawful"[27] slavery, a groundbreaking decision in its day.

Legal scholars consider *Swift v. Tyson*, an 1842 case, Story's most important opinion. *Swift* involved cases heard in federal court brought in diversity jurisdiction—disputes between citizens of different states. Story ruled that federal courts could decide matters not specifically addressed by state legislatures, granting federal courts authority to develop federal common law, greater than states' common law.

Joseph Story's impact, however, was more as sage and scholar than as judge.

In chapter 1 I discussed Sir Edward Coke collecting judicial decisions of prior ages with the intent to bring order to English law. Chapter 4, "1612: *Case of Sutton's Hospital*," reviewed Sir Francis Bacon's creation of the scientific method. Story combined both concepts on a massive scale, called *applied law*, using the order of physical sciences to organize the law.

Today, legal practice guides are taken for granted. Consider that 1817 was Harvard Law School's first class. In the 1820s, particularly in the western states, the sharing of statute books was just commencing, and access to scholarly journals was scarce. How were American lawyers to know what was the accepted law of the judges who came before them? English authority still counted after independence but was no longer binding. The subject of American law and practice was a work in progress, with most of the building blocks scattered about.

Also, America was changing. During the 1820s the country experienced a rising tide of populism culminating with Andrew Jackson's election as president in 1828. Historians call this period "The Age of Jackson." Control of the federal government fell to a band of ill-mannered and semi-literate Jackson followers. Joseph Story was concerned about the altering political climate. He feared that the Jacksonians would disregard the law for their own corrupt ends. The purpose and foundation of the law had to be made known.

During this time, Story was offered an endowed chair to teach law at Harvard. So he joined the faculty while still sitting on the Supreme Court. The High Court simply did not provide enough work to keep Story's superior mind occupied. Harvard had twelve law students in 1829. It's difficult to fathom the potential of a small group of bright soon-to-be lawyers taught by the unbridled mind of Joseph Story.

Between 1832 and 1845 Story published eleven volumes of sweeping legal commentaries, attempting to impose scientific order upon American jurisprudence. In 1835 he published his two-volume treatise, *Commentaries on Equity Jurisprudence: As Administered in England and America*. An instant success, it was reprinted twelve times by 1918. His brilliant mind was financially rewarded, which should be an inspiration to entrepreneurs everywhere. It does not always happen that way.

In 1838 Story published a sequel, *Commentaries on Equity Pleadings, and the Incidents Thereof: According to the Practice of the Courts of Equity, of America and England*. This treatise was more nuts and bolts than the lofty principles of the prior publication, providing even the form that equity proceedings should follow. This publication was reprinted eight times before 1892—another successful business venture.

As the nation's preeminent and certainly most productive legal scholar, he was also the author of *Commentaries on the Law of Bailments* (1832), *Commentaries on the Constitution of the United States* (three volumes, 1833), *Commentaries on the Conflict of Laws: Foreign and Domestic* (1834), *Commentaries on the Law of Agency* (1839), *Commentaries on the Law of Partnership* (1841), *Commentaries on the Law of Bills of Exchange* (1843), and *Commentaries on the Law of Promissory Notes* (1845). These writings contributed mightily to the emergence of what he called "the modern legal textbook."

It was said that Justice Story could write a commentary quicker than a lawyer could read it. And he did all this while also writing 286 opinions as a Supreme Court associate justice.

Story's books Americanized and modernized issues of common law and equity. His many different commentary treatises, containing the critical precedential material that is the basis of our common law system, were among the bestselling books of the first half of the nineteenth century and treated as the "code" of legal principles used by judges and lawyers in the budding American frontier that lacked law libraries. These writings formed the basis of wide-ranging insight into the role of law in American society and provided historical context from English common law. Indeed, these treatises are so influential that many basic rules of state law can be traced back in their case law to Justice Story's original citations. British courts continue to cite his work to this day!

Story wrote his *Commentaries* in part to counter his concern about the rise of The Age of Jackson. America needed clear guidance regarding formalized legal principles as opposed to ruinous mob mentality.

Commentaries on Equity Jurisprudence was, as Story put it, an exposition of the leading principles of "an important branch of the science of law."[28] This was an age of system building. Story searched legal writings from ancient Rome to contemporary Philadelphia in search of "the law." I bet Sir Edward Coke, the boorish writer of the famed *Reports* establishing the model of English "legal precedent," might have even cracked a guarded smile. But Story went even further. Why not apply the scientific ordering concepts to law, particularly rules of equity, wherever the common law was powerless? Otherwise, the law would cease to be effective. The methodology and order of the physical sciences had to be applied to the universe of law. Sir Francis Bacon's soul is ecstatic!

I'd love to see an aspiring novelist write a book imagining a meeting between Sir Francis Bacon, who lived two hundred years prior, and the Honorable Joseph Story. Picture these two legal giants of different ages and from different countries meeting in a fantastic library to discuss and compare not just the content of the law but each one's way of studying it. We might not understand all their intellectual interactions, but it would make for a fascinating conversation.

Equity principles usually sound lofty. Justice Story is often credited with the line, "He who seeks equity must do equity," from his *Equity Jurisprudence*.[29] I'm told every lawyer should know this basic maxim of law. The phrase guided legions and generations of judges and attorneys prior to the formalization of these concepts into statutes. Other basic concepts of equity include the following:

- Those who come to equity must come with clean hands.
- Equity regards as done that which ought to be done.
- Equity follows the law.
- Delay defeats equity.

Seems like simple stuff, but like anything in the law, it all gets complicated. So judges and lawyers need hefty *Commentaries*.

Justice Story's *Commentaries on Equity Pleadings* and *Equity Jurisprudence* are credited as effectively creating the foundation of American class action law. Story deemed the "representative suit" as an exception to the rule governing joinder of necessary parties.

Admittedly, Story's concepts regarding representative suits were preliminary, rough, and maybe even hesitant. He didn't have a lot of American experience as fodder for his writings.

At the turn of the twentieth century, John Pomeroy's *Equity* gradually replaced Story's as the standard reference treatise. But successor Pomeroy complimented Story's treatise as "one of the few American law books that is frequently cited by the English courts."[30]

As you will see in chapter 12, "1936: The Birth of Grandfather 23," Story's concepts guided Professor J. W. Moore, the controlling author of the original Federal Rules of Civil Procedure of 1938. Story's categorization of disputes excusing joinder of numerous, necessary parties involved questions of "common or general" interest, the involvement of voluntary associations, and the concept that when parties are so numerous, without regard to other standards, joinder is impractical. These remain among the standard modes of analysis for class action cases. Story's classifications of representative suits, later to be called "class suits," are still the structural groundwork of our modern Federal Rules of Civil Procedure rule 23.

Consider this passage:

> "All persons materially interested in the subject-matter [of the suit] ought to be [joined]," with exceptions that joinder will be excused in situations in which it is impracticable, and when "as to parties . . . where they are exceedingly numerous, and it would be impracticable to join them without almost interminable delays and other inconveniences. . . . In such cases, the Court . . . will dispense with them . . . if it can be done without injury to the persons not actually before the Court."
>
> Joseph Story, *Commentaries on Equity Pleadings* (1838)

This has a familiar ring to those in the class action world, doesn't it?

Some of Story's relevant analyses were concerned with the *res judicata* effect on absentee "Necessary Parties." While modern-day judges still grapple with class action certification and settlement issues' effect on "absentee" parties, we now call these people *class members*, and class action administrators are charged with locating and providing notice, conveniences unavailable before the Civil War. Justice Story opined, "[I]ndeed, in most, if not in all, cases of this sort, the decree obtained upon such a Bill will ordinarily be held binding upon all other persons standing in the same predicament."[31]

Res judicata, also known as claim preclusion, refers to a case in which there has been a final judgment and the case is no longer subject to appeal. It is meant to bar (or preclude) re-litigation of a claim between the same parties.

"Same predicament" is a gentle, nineteenth-century way to discuss commonality or typicality. Story illustrated this with the example of a miller possessing a monopoly, requiring all residents of a region to use his mill. He argued the miller could sue a few inhabitants to determine his rights against them all, just as we saw in Olde England.

Joseph Story died in 1845 at age sixty-five, after thirty-three years on the Supreme Court. While considering retirement, Story had also planned to write additional books on shipping, insurance, equity practice, admiralty, and public international law. His volumes on equity continued to be the preeminent legal authority until after 1900. Though Justice Story's role in the formation of American jurisprudence is underappreciated today, he was undoubtedly among the most prolific American legal writers in our history.

In the early 1800s Story was one of the most successful writers of his day—writing law books that sold like iPhones upon their first release. He remains an icon of constitutional scholars, a preeminent player in the history of group representation lawsuits, and the grandfather of modern class actions. Hopefully, this chapter about his life and prolific works has illustrated his vast contribution to our nation's laws.

In 1938 the U.S. Supreme Court, in the landmark *Erie Railroad Co. v. Tompkins* decision, authored by the esteemed Louis Brandeis, found that federal courts did not have the power to create federal common law when hearing state law claims under diversity jurisdiction. After almost one hundred years, Story's *Swift v. Tyson* opinion was reversed.

Today a few states still operate distinct and separate equity courts. Equity rules have mostly been codified and written into statutes passed by Congress, state legislatures, or, frequently, in the case of class actions, the Federal Advisory Committee.

In 1997 Supreme Court Associate Justice Harry Blackmun, author of *Roe v. Wade*, played the role of Justice Joseph Story in Steven Spielberg's *Amistad*, starring Academy Award–winning actors Morgan Freeman and Anthony Hopkins. The scenes of courtroom drama in the movie were the only known time that a sitting justice played another member of the court in the movies.

Chapter 9

1845: *Smith v. Swormstedt*—The South Secedes

But does not this question [slavery] make a disturbance outside of political circles? Does it not enter the churches and rend them asunder? What divided the great Methodist Church into two parts, North and South?

Has anything ever threatened the existence of this Union save and except this very institution of slavery?
—Abraham Lincoln, Lincoln-Douglas Debates,
October 15, 1858, Alton, Illinois

Before the Methodist church split in 1845, as stated by then-senatorial candidate Abraham Lincoln above, it was the largest organization in America outside of the federal government. Both sides of the splintered group were high-spirited, driven by the national religious revival known as the Second Great Awakening and with their passionately held beliefs on each side of the slavery debate. This division led to the first major U.S. Supreme Court group representation case, with many parties from different states fighting over entitlements to a separate organizational relief fund for itinerant preachers and their families.

John Wesley, founder of the Methodist Movement, was ordained as an Anglican priest in 1728. In 1738 he started his movement within the Church of England, based on the concept of *methodism*, meaning a methodical pursuit of biblical holiness. His Christian revival approach broke many existing norms of the church. By 1770, as a matter of policy, Methodist clergy weren't permitted to own slaves. A leading-edge thinker in 1771, Wesley started permitting women to become lay preachers. During this time, he became a highly active abolitionist, preaching against slavery and the slave trade, both in the colonies and in Britain. Threats of violence and attacks against Wesley by mobs were becoming the norm.

After the American Revolution, Northern Methodists continued to oppose slavery. They regularly sent ministers to the South to preach "free your slaves," seeing limited success from their efforts. Around that time, Wesley set up a "Yearly Conference of the People Called Methodists" so his approach to the ministry would survive after his death. However, while he always considered himself part of the Anglican Church, the Church of England was unenthusiastic about retaining him and his followers.

Wesley died in 1791. It took only four years for his followers to create a separate Methodist church. Soon thereafter, in America, the church created a charitable fund called the Methodist Book Concern, devoted to publishing and selling religious books. The profits went to support traveling church preachers, their wives, widows, children, and orphans. The fund was founded and primarily financed by sales of these books made by traveling preachers. The funds never belonged to the church, but the church managed and controlled them.

When the church split on the slavery issue, monies earned from the Book Concern became the subject of the largest group representation lawsuit to reach the U.S. Supreme Court in the nineteenth century.

During the 1830s two great movements—one economic, one spiritual—were in full throttle. Cotton was a massive industry, ruling the South's economy. Cotton is easy to grow, and unlike most farm products, it preserves well. However, removing the seeds was exceedingly difficult and time-consuming. Eli Whitney's cotton gin solved this problem, completely changing the South's economic landscape. Cotton became king and the need for cheap labor, in the form of slaves, grew in economic importance.

Alexis de Tocqueville, famed French sociologist, political theorist, and author of the 1835 classic *Democracy in America,* which detailed his extensive observations in the New World, wrote that there existed "no country in the whole world in which the Christian religion retains a greater influence over the souls of men than in America."[32] This revivalist spirit sweeping the country benefited Methodist and Baptist churches more than other denominations.

Superimposed over these two omnipotent forces was Lincoln's "question" of slavery. In 1831 Nat Turner led a slave revolt resulting in the death of fifty-five Whites in a single day. The uprising caused White fear and a serious anti-abolitionist backlash in the South, including harsh laws preventing slaves from being able to assemble, hold religious meetings without a licensed White minister present, or even be taught to read and write. Abolitionists were forced to flee the South for their lives.

Northern Methodist abolitionists considered slavery the most daunting barrier to the state of perfection in society, the goal of all evangelical hopes. The Lord's love for humanity and the promotion of social causes were underlying principles of Scripture. Slavery was an attack on the American social order, the antithesis of the declared values of democratic institutions. In response, Southern church leaders developed scriptural defenses of slavery, pointing to the Bible's literal language. Slavery was commonplace among the Israelites. There is no quote from Jesus condemning slavery. Paul the apostle even returned a slave to his master (Philemon 1:12).

The schism along geographical lines between the Methodist and Baptist faiths, the nation's two largest Protestant denominations, not only foretold the political split of the 1860s but is considered a leading cause. The broken social bonds between two great religious organizations created an environment justifying, supporting, and rationalizing political separation.

We all know that it took a horrible war that claimed more than six hundred thousand American lives to finally settle the slavery question.

By the 1840s America was changing. In 1841 *The Amistad* case, discussed in the previous chapter, was decided—a win in the abolitionist force's column. Inherently important for any "group representation" history was the 1842 creation of Equity Rule 48, the forerunner of our present-day Federal Rule of Civil Procedure rule 23 governing class actions (first introduced in 1938). It stated:

> Where the parties on either side are very numerous, and cannot, without manifest inconvenience and oppressive delays in the suit, be all brought before it, the court in its discretion may dispense with making all of them parties, and may proceed in the suit, having sufficient parties before it to represent all the adverse interests of the plaintiffs and defendants in the suit properly before it. But in such cases the decree shall be without prejudice to the rights and claims of all the absent parties.[33]

I'll talk more about this later when I discuss the lawsuit, but consider the spirit of America at the time. In 1843 the first wagon train of nine hundred settlers, called *immigrants*, set off on the Oregon Trail. In 1844 the first telegraph message, using Morse Code, was sent between Baltimore and Washington, D.C. In 1845 the United States annexed Texas, and President James Polk announced America's "Manifest Destiny." Of equal importance to some, the inventors of the rubber band obtained their patent.

Also, in 1845, the Methodist Church split in two.

The ultimate dispute arose in the General Conference convened in New York City on May 1, 1844. The six-week session was the longest General Conference in Methodist church history, continuing the annual meeting originally set up by John Wesley.

The spark igniting the ultimate division arose when Bishop James Andrew of Georgia married, causing unique marital issues. Andrew's new wife inherited slaves from her late husband. Northern Methodists were appalled at a Methodist bishop owning slaves. The discipline for the Methodist Church states that a Methodist bishop cannot buy and sell slaves. Bishop Andrew argued that he didn't buy or sell slaves; they were received through marriage. Moreover, as possessions, the slaves were in his wife's name, and she could do with them as she saw fit. "I have neither bought nor sold a slave," he told the General Conference. "In the state where I am legally a slaveholder, emancipation is impracticable."[34]

Bishop Andrew's "slaveholding" didn't end there. Fanning the flames was his inheritance of another slave from a woman in Augusta, Georgia. A local church member asked the bishop to care for a slave girl until she turned nineteen. Then he was to emancipate her and send her off to Liberia. However, if the slave girl didn't want to go to Liberia, the bishop was alternatively directed to make her "as free as the laws of Georgia would permit." The young woman didn't want to go to Liberia. She continued living in her own house on the bishop's lot. She was free to go north if she wished, but until then, she was legally his slave. There was nothing he could do to end this situation as the woman's wishes and Georgia law prevented him from any other course of action.

It's fair to say that Northern abolitionists were not persuaded by Bishop Andrew's excuses for slaveholding when the Lord's calling in Scripture was involved. After twelve days of debate, all efforts at compromise failed.

The 1845 dispute led to the church split, or the creation of a new church, depending on the parties' legal perspectives. This new entity was called Methodist Episcopal Church South. Local conferences throughout the South sent delegates to a convention in Louisville in May 1845, where this new church entity was formed.

After this division and the creation of a new entity was defined, the Southern church sought its pro rata shares of the Book Concern funds on behalf of the traveling ministers and their families. This was the genesis of *Smith v. Swormstedt*, the first seminal U.S. Supreme Court class action.

The historical church, now of the North, replied with a definitive *no*. The South voluntarily abandoned the organization. The North claimed it never agreed to allocate funds to the new entity. The Southern church disagreed, arguing the Methodists had divided their church and the new body was entitled to their share. The U.S. Supreme Court ultimately agreed with the Southern church.

The complainants were, of course, interested in obtaining their share of the Book Concern funds for the Southern preachers and their families. The defendants were the Northern traveling preachers, those overseeing the Book Concern.

Sadly, there is no surviving record of the briefs or arguments in the case due to its age. We do, however, have the Supreme Court's opinion, which defines the class:

> As to those whom they choose to represent, they say, "That there are about fifteen hundred preachers belonging to the travelling connection of the Methodist Episcopal Church South, each of whom has a direct personal interest in the same right as your complainants to the said property.

The complainants also aver, that this bill is brought by the authority, and under the direction of the general and annual conferences of the church south, and for the benefit of the same, and for themselves, and all the preachers in the travelling connection, and all other ministers and persons having an interest in the property.[35]

The claimants' counsel, however, went a creative step further, suing the Northern defendant traveling preachers' beneficiaries as a group while including them within the plaintiff class. They had the same interest in the fund, and "in view of sustaining a just decision in the matter, to make them all parties to the bill." Amazing. The lawyers for the Southern preachers were suing the Northern preachers but also appreciated that the Northerners also had rights and interest in the fund and a fair resolution could not be adjudicated without including them as well. So they were defendants and beneficiaries at the same time.

The Supreme Court's opinion citing "Mr. Justice Story, in his valuable treatise on Equity Pleadings,"[36] was a wide endorsement of class action principles that would later come into common acceptance.

> The rule is well established, where the parties interested are numerous, and the suit is for an object common to them all, some of the body may maintain a bill on behalf of themselves and of the others; and a bill may also be maintained against a portion of a numerous body of defendants, representing a common interest.

As to issues of numerosity, the court stated:

> The rights of the several persons may be separate and distinct, yet there must be a common interest or a common right, which the bill seeks to establish or enforce. As an illustration, bills have been permitted to be brought by the lord of a manor against some of the tenants, and *vice versa*, by some of the tenants in behalf of themselves and the other tenants, to establish some right—such as suit to a mill, or right of common, or to cut turf. So by a parson of

a parish against some of the parishioners to establish a general right to tithes—or conversely, by some of the parishioners in behalf of all to establish a parochial modus.

The legal and equitable rights and liabilities of all being before the court by representation, and especially where the subject-matter of the suit is common to all, there can be very little danger but that the interest of all will be properly protected and maintained.[37]

Aren't you glad you read the Olde English chapters now?

In *Smith v. Swormstedt*, there were about fifteen hundred persons represented by the complainants. Smith was a Methodist Episcopal Church South commissioner appointed to represent his similarly situated ministers. Swormstedt was an agent of the Book of Concern. The defendants represented about three thousand persons. The court found that to not include everyone in the same lawsuit "would amount to a denial of justice"—the essence of equity.

This was, then, the first time that the U.S. Supreme Court established the possibility of binding effects of lawsuits in group representation litigation on absent group members. That is, the Court declared that every person affected by this decision, whether they had signed onto the case or even knew it was happening, was entitled to compensation.

But wait! There's more! Consider the fact that Equity Rule 48 was enacted just a few years prior, with its final sentence stating, ". . . but in such cases the decree shall be without prejudice to the rights and claims of all the absent parties." However, *Swormstedt* included the absent parties within the opinion anyway. The Supreme Court simply ignored its new Equity Rule 48. Why? How?

Those far-ranging implications go beyond my self-appointed storytelling role. It's just something for wise men and women reading this tale to chew on.

Swormstedt's historical link between the policies underlying the early equity practice and modern class action rules is similar to Sir

Edward Coke's dissertation in the case of Sutton's Hospital (chapter 4). English equity courts had long developed representative actions, facilitating more efficient ways to adjudicate disputes in multiparty litigation. *Swormstedt* employed representative actions for "convenience . . . and to prevent a failure of justice."

The Supreme Court awarded attorney fees and costs to both sides, to be paid from the Book Concern funds. The trial court was directed to appoint a master to perform an accounting and determine how much to allocate to each entity. The Southern entity received 6 percent interest on the unpaid balances. No class action administration industry existed back then. That would take another hundred years.

Federal Equity Rule 48 remained the law until 1912 with scant judicial mention of the inconsistencies between the rule and the *Swormstedt* opinion. It was rewritten into Equity Rule 38 in 1912, allowing absent parties to be included in judgments under the law.

The Methodist Church remained separated until 1939, when it finally reunited.

The United Methodist Church remains the largest Protestant denomination in America with at least one church in every county in America. However, in 2024 the issue of same-sex marriage and the ordination of LGBTQ pastors caused another official church realignment, permitting congregations to vote whether to leave the denomination over these issues.

Smith v. Swormstedt lives on. It remains a point of reference in the authoritative Federal Rules Advisory Committee Notes, a guide for lawyers to find additional meaning to the Rules. Also, federal courts have cited *Swormstedt* about a dozen times in the last decade. The decision's influence still lingers.

Chapter 10

1920: The Tribe of Ben-Hur

In the nature of things Freedom and Slavery cannot be coexistent. I could not bring myself to defend the institution of slavery, my sympathies would side with the fugitive against his master. In all nature was nothing more natural than the yearning for freedom.
—Lew Wallace: An Autobiography, Volume 1, *1906*

In the cold and dreary February of 1862, the Civil War had been raging for almost a year. During that time there had been scant Union victories. Northerners needed a strategic, emotional boost, a clear victory in battle.

Ulysses S. Grant, Union brigadier general, had a plan: Retake control of the Mississippi River and divide the South geographically and economically by commanding the critical shipping lane of the great and powerful river.

Vicksburg was the prize; the fortress overlooked the mighty Mississippi. An attack from the river was impracticable, maybe impossible.

Strategically, to lay siege on Vicksburg, the Union had to first take Jackson, the Mississippi state capital. The army's path took them straight through Tennessee on their way to northern Mississippi.

The first goal was gaining control of the Cumberland and Tennessee Rivers, passageways from neutral Western Kentucky to Rebel Tennessee. These routes were critical for transporting supplies south to gain control of Nashville. Two Rebel forts constructed on these rivers stood in the way: Fort Henry on the Tennessee and Fort Donelson on the Cumberland.

Major General Lew Wallace's Indiana Regiment was under Grant's command. Wallace was no stranger to war. In 1846, at the outbreak of the Mexican-American War, Wallace was only nineteen years old. At this tender age, the young lad raised a company of volunteers, fought in General Zachary Taylor's army, and attained the rank of first lieutenant. Capable, courageous, and commanding, Wallace certainly had fighting chops along with smarts. His intellect and impact ignited a series of circumstances leading to a most seminal U.S. Supreme Court decision seventy-five years later.

At the onset of the Civil War, Wallace was practicing law when he was called upon to raise the 11th Indiana Volunteer Infantry Regiment. He accomplished the task in one week. War fever was running high. Wallace had limited success in early skirmishes in Maryland and present-day West Virginia. To institute Grant's plan, Wallace was assigned to lead a regiment in Tennessee. But Wallace grew restless as his forces were held in reserve, away from the fighting.

Fort Henry was poorly situated on low, swampy ground. No better strategic location existed due to the nature of the terrain. Heavy, cold rains flooded the fort. After less than two hours of Union gunboats' fire, the fort fell. The Stars and Stripes again flew in Tennessee. Grant ordered Wallace's Indiana regiment to take positions at Fort Donelson.

After following those orders, an admiral casually invited Wallace to join a Navy reconnaissance mission up the Tennessee River. It was a simple "Let's go take a look at Donelson." The sailors spotted a fugitive slave on the shore frantically fleeing bloodhounds and horsemen in hot pursuit. Wallace had heard of hunting slaves with hounds but had never personally witnessed it. The cruel chase after the runaway incensed Wallace. He wanted to kill the pursuers and joined the crew firing shots at the slave hunters. A boat was ordered to rescue the unfortunate freedom-seeking slave, who had climbed a tree, with his bare feet and ankles dangling just out of reach of the menacing, growling dogs. The sailors ultimately drove off the predatory canines with their oars.

Wallace had freed his first slave.

Grant's army of almost seventeen thousand men took Fort Donelson. Confederate General Simon Bolivar Buckner was inside. When attending West Point together, Grant and Buckner had become awfully close friends. Their friendship was reinforced by the camaraderie and trust forged in the tension and excitement of the Mexican-American War. Grant had left the army in 1854 and later found himself in New York City, unable to pay for his return trip to his family in Ohio. By sheer coincidence, he ran into his old war buddy Buckner, who loaned the now-penniless ex-captain enough money to return home.

Back at Fort Donelson, Buckner sought a path to free his army from certain capture. But heavy politics intervened. Confederate General John B. Floyd in Donelson had been President James Buchanan's secretary of war. However, he was seemingly more concerned about his own fate than victory, as he was accused after Lincoln's election of sending large amounts of government arms from Federal arsenals to the Rebels. He was afraid that, if captured, he'd be tried for treason and hanged. Command of the entire fort was left to Buckner, while other commanders planned their escape with a small group of men.

Buckner also attempted a daring escape, his soldiers successfully pushing back on Wallace's lines. However, Wallace reconstituted his command, forcing Buckner's army back to the fort. Wallace was credited with holding this stalemate. Buckner pleaded to Grant, his old friend, for terms of surrender.

In response, Grant stated, in his now historical letter, "No terms except an unconditional and immediate surrender can be accepted. I propose to move immediately upon your works."[38] For his stern response, and not permitting a genial, strong friendship to interfere with the business of war and his obligations as a U.S. Army officer, Grant became known as "Unconditional Surrender Grant," a play on his initials, U. S. Grant.

Buckner, a Southern gentleman, expected a higher degree of cordiality from his longtime friend. But this was a time of war.

At Donelson, Grant captured more prisoners than the combined Union army had taken to date: an impressive 13,500 men, along with his old friend and fifty other Confederate field officers. Wallace witnessed Buckner personally surrender to Grant, the first time a Confederate general surrendered his army.

The first major Union victories at Forts Henry and Donelson provided Northerners a much-needed emotional boost regarding the war effort. Wallace, then thirty-four years old, was promoted to major general for his military prowess in aiding those early victories. He was the youngest Union general at the time.

Once inside Donelson, Wallace read abandoned Rebel soldiers' mail, hoping to find military intelligence he could act upon. Instead, Wallace found letters of family members demonstrating the extent of their dedication to the secessionist cause. He was previously unaware of their fierce loyalty. These letters, along with his adversaries' gallant fighting in the field, was later found to influence his approach to writing about Roman soldiers in his fictional masterpiece and unprecedented best seller, *Ben-Hur: A Tale of the Christ*. As I'll explain later, *The Tribe of Ben Hur* was the plaintiff in the monumental U.S. Supreme Court class action.

Buckner spent six months in a Massachusetts prisoner of war camp, before being released in a prisoner exchange, returning to fight for the Rebel cause until the end of the war. In June 1865 he was the last Confederate general to surrender forces at the conflict's termination, two months after Lee's surrender to Grant at Appomattox Court House.

Grant's plan of invasion next led to the Battle of Shiloh, forever to be remembered as "Deadly Shiloh," with more casualties than any other prior conflict in American history. Indeed, twice as many souls were lost in this battle than in the entire war to date. Wallace fought well at the two-day battle; however, he was accused of disregarding orders, leading to greater losses. Due to confusion on the battlefield, caused in part by verbal instead of written orders, Wallace was perhaps a little stubborn and allegedly took his regiment on a different road than the one ordered. The result? He was temporarily removed from active duty and transferred from Grant's command, damaging his military career. However, he is still recognized for his successful September 1862 defense of Cincinnati, Ohio, then the sixth-largest city in America.

Wallace is also credited for his shielding of Washington, D.C, in the July 1864 Battle of Monocacy. Even though Wallace was forced to retreat and is considered to have lost that battle, he helped save the capital by slowing the Rebel's advance and allowing time for reinforcements to arrive.

Wallace's standing was high at the end of the war. He was appointed to serve on the military commission investigating the conspirators in President Lincoln's assassination. With the war finally over, Wallace returned to his native Indiana, heralded as a great Hoosier hero in

Crawfordsville. But he was apparently not popular enough; he was twice defeated when running for Congress in 1868 and 1870.

In 1873 Wallace published his first historical novel, *The Fair God*, which focused on Cortez's conquest of Mexico. He had begun writing it thirty years earlier. It sold seven thousand copies in its first year, which was quite admirable, particularly back then. That same year, Wallace began researching *Ben-Hur: A Tale of the Christ*, an ultimate blockbuster bestseller centered around a Jewish nobleman's life during those times, witnessing events leading up to and including Jesus' crucifixion.

In 1878 President Rutherford B. Hayes appointed Wallace territorial governor of New Mexico. The Palace of the Governors in Santa Fe, constructed by the Spanish, had been the seat of New Mexico government since 1610. While governing, Wallace completed writing *Ben-Hur* there during the evenings under the glow of a gas lantern. The Palace remains a national landmark. Does it sound like a peaceful life after years in the thick of battle? Not entirely. Wallace was charged with ending the "Lincoln County War," a series of revenge killings, combined with seeking control of valuable cattle and sheep ranging lands in distant areas of the New Mexico Territory.

Enter the infamous Billy the Kid.

Outlaw Billy was a lead protagonist in the Lincoln County Wars. Many in his day (and today) would say that he acted at least in part out of his own sense of frontier justice. He saw himself as a freedom fighter. Indeed, many locals supported him and provided him necessary protection. Since the Kid was concerned about justice, he wrote Governor Wallace about witnessing the brutal murder of an attorney friend, stating, "I was present when Mr. Chapman was murdered."[39] Billy sought protection and a pardon for all his prior wrongs. A secret rendezvous was arranged. Wallace, the hardened warrior, was unafraid. The governor knew that he was the Kid's only hope for a pardon.

Wallace offered Billy a full pardon if he would testify. The deal was struck. A plan was devised. The Kid was to be arrested and jailed for his own protection. Billy testified as agreed, but the scales of New Mexico frontier justice were not equally balanced; the deck was stacked, and the defendants were acquitted—and Billy the Kid was still sitting in jail. The local district attorney revoked Billy's bargain with Governor Wallace, refusing to set him free. Living up to his legend, however, Billy somehow managed to kill two guards and escape. This was followed by another killing spree, often based on revenge, which has since been made famous in books and movies.

Wallace then signed a new death warrant for Billy, ordering the gathering of a posse that included Sheriff Pat Garrett. Soon thereafter, Wallace stepped aboard the New York–bound train to meet the publisher Harper & Brothers, holding his handwritten, completed *Ben-Hur* manuscript.

After four months of tracking, Pat Garrett found and killed Billy the Kid.

Ben-Hur was published in November 1880. During the first five years, sales were slow, but mildly respectful. In March 1881 Wallace resigned his territorial governor post and was assigned as U.S. minister to the Ottoman Empire, serving in Constantinople, modern-day Istanbul, until 1885. By 1886 sales of *Ben Hur* had grown, as about fifty thousand copies were sold each year.

Finally, there was an explosion of unprecedented sales. In 1893 his seminal work was the most popular book borrowed from public libraries. Nice to know that they kept track of those things back then. Just before the turn of the century, *Ben-Hur* surpassed Harriet Beecher Stowe's *Uncle Tom's Cabin* as the best-selling American novel of the nineteenth century. By 1912 one million copies were sold. In 1913 Sears, Roebuck and Company ordered a million copies, the largest single print edition in U.S. history at the time.

During the 1890s "the Gilded Age" was in full gear. America was experiencing rapid economic growth driven by railroads, factories, mining, and finance. In 1886 former President Hayes wrote in his diary, "It is a government by the corporations, of the corporations, and for the corporations."

Immigrants from Europe poured in. Corruption and large-scale con men were everywhere. Former President Grant fell victim to an unfortunate scam by his most trusted business partner. Life insurance companies fell under the ambience of widespread corruption as well.

Back home in Indiana, Lew Wallace, famed war hero and author, was approached by the good folks of his hometown of Crawfordsville with a grand idea. In response to the rampant corruption of the times, they desired to create a genuine fraternal beneficial society controlled by the entire membership. The organization, they argued, would provide a unique breed of mutual life insurance with the preeminent purpose of offering death benefits to appointed beneficiaries from assessments paid by its members. They came to General Wallace with a wish to name the association the Knights of Ben-Hur in honor of his grand novel.

Wallace must have paused and said words to the effect of "No! The knights didn't arrive in the lexicon of history until later during the Middle Ages." He suggested instead the *Tribe* of Ben-Hur. The change was happily accepted by the organizers. The roots and naming rights of this class action classic were set into formation.

This wasn't a simple association such as being a member of the Automobile Club, AARP, or REI. The intent and practice were a true fraternal association, replete with rituals and secret oaths, groups organized to study Wallace's masterpiece, degrees conferred, and events arranged with costumed characters from the novel singing and dancing scenes from *Ben-Hur*. Junior Ben-Hur "orders" were created akin to the Boy Scouts and Girl Scouts. A full official consumer line of special badges, charms, memorial spoons—even a scholarship program—were all part of the Tribe of Ben-Hur association.

The officers included the ex-governor of Indiana, a judge, the mayor of Crawfordsville, and a Methodist pastor. The titles of officers included Supreme Judge, Supreme Keeper of Tribute, Supreme Medical Examiner, and the Supreme Keepers of the Inner and Outer Gates. Wallace was a full participatory member. The novel's overwhelming popularity spread the legitimacy of the Order.

By 1896 'courts' were held in a dozen states with a total membership of approximately five thousand. In this circumstance, 'courts' meant a gathering of tribal members. It was an associational meeting of sorts, not in any way a legal court proceeding. By 1905 fifteen hundred courts were held in twenty-six states with more than a hundred thousand members.

Eventually, like many fads or crazes, interest and membership began to recede. Younger potential members were cautious about joining, concerned about simply subsidizing older members, with their younger members designated beneficiaries potentially seeing no compensation. Actuarial naiveté plagued many friendly societies at this time. Younger members were faced with a distinctly less advantageous schedule of benefits. Widespread trouble and animosity were stirring in the Tribe.

In 1908 the Tribe considered bankruptcy. Instead, to attract new members, two classes of membership were created. Older members were designated as Class A, and younger members as Class B. The two classes paid different rates. Class A members' rates rose, and the funds were kept separate. The inexpensive insurance of the past for this group ceased because it would no longer be subsidized by the Class B new members. Also, fraternal organizations at this time had no reserve funds requirements standard like conventional life insurance companies. Therefore, the fund could only remain solvent if new members continued to join. Smell that class action looming?

Since we have lots of people from different states and a monumental Supreme Court decision brewing, a quick discussion of "diversity jurisdiction" is required for non-lawyers. In 1789, during the very first session of Congress, federal court diversity jurisdiction was created. The concern was that of defendants being *home-towned*, meaning a plaintiff might want to file a lawsuit in their home state court (not the local federal court). Defendants might experience a natural bias against them as the lowly out-of-staters. This diversity rule allowed an out-of-state defendant to challenge state court jurisdiction on those grounds and to force the matter to federal court if no plaintiffs were from the same state as any defendant. This rule remains in force to this day.

Now, the legal action commences.

The first lawsuit hit in 1913. Five years after the Tribe's reorganization, *non-Indianans* challenged it, bringing a class action *in Indiana federal district court*. They sued the Indiana corporation in federal diversity jurisdiction. These suits typically contested the right of the

Logo of the Supreme Tribe of Ben-Hur, Crawfordsville, Indiana, early twentieth century.

association to raise assessments to pay death benefits as their membership grew older and to cancel certificates when members failed to pay increased assessments. In total, 524 plaintiffs sued on the basis that their vested contract rights were violated. The plaintiffs lost.

The obvious unfairness of the situation increased. Due to the sheer number of other potential members involved, it was virtually assured that the courts would be forced to litigate the same issues again and again. As a result, courts were obliged to decide whether a prior judgment in a class suit barred a later suit by someone not actually a party to the judgment.

The second lawsuit came in 1919. Aurelia Cauble and other members of Class A—*all Indiana citizens*—brought another class action suit *in Indiana state court*, essentially with the same challenge as in the first lawsuit. But Ms. Cauble and others similarly situated were not parties or even aware of the previous lawsuit. How could she and other class members be bound by the decision in the first lawsuit?

Beneficial Certificate of the Supreme Tribe of Ben-Hur, Arkansas, 1924.

Then the third lawsuit came in 1920. The Supreme Tribe of Ben Hur *moved in federal court* for an injunction against the second suit, claiming preclusion based on the first. I bet that Sir Edward Coke would be upset that the Tribe brought an injunction action in equity to halt the state court proceedings. Defendant Cauble argued that whatever binding effect the earlier class suit had on non-Indiana residents, she wasn't bound because her Indiana citizenship defeated the federal court's diversity jurisdiction had she been an actual party to the suit.

The District Court agreed with Ms. Cauble and the other defendants. The U.S. Supreme Court reversed.

In 1921 the High Court was faced with the difficult issue of barring absent class members in subsequent litigation against the issue of the multitude of continuing similar suits, along with the diversity issue. They cited Equity Rule 38, promulgated in 1912, which stated:

> When the question is one of common or general interest to many persons constituting a class so numerous as to make it impracticable to bring them all before the court, one or more may sue or defend for the whole.[40]

The court found that "a class suit of this nature might have been maintained in a state court and would have been binding on all of the class, we can have no doubt."[41] Finding the rights of Mrs. Cauble and her class

> were duly represented by those before the federal court . . . Being thus represented, we think it must necessarily follow that their rights were concluded by the original decree [and that] the decree when rendered must bind all of the class properly represented.[42]

The High Court's opinion was couched in terms of resolving the federal jurisdictional issue looking only at the citizenship of the class representatives, not the membership.

The *Ben-Hur* decision is quoted in the Federal Rule of Civil Procedure Rule 23 1966 Advisory Committee Notes, and although it is occasionally criticized, it is still an important Supreme Court precedent.

Over the years, the Supreme Tribe of Ben-Hur association succumbed to the pressures of Internal Revenue Service fraternal organization nontaxable status issues, moving to become a commercial

Lew Wallace, author of Ben-Hur: A Tale of the Christ, *writing under the Ben-Hur beech, late nineteenth century.*

company. Today the successor entity of the Ben-Hur fraternal organization is a commercial company, USA Life Insurance Company of Indiana, created in 1988.

The remains of Fort Henry were permanently submerged in the 1930s during the Tennessee Valley Authority's damming and electrification projects. Fort Donelson remains as a National Park Battlefield site.

Lew Wallace built a fantastic personal study back home in Crawfordsville from his *Ben-Hur* proceeds. It cost $30,000 to build—an astounding cost at the time. The structure is designated as a National Historic Landmark. Wallace wrote seven other books, most notably *The Prince of India: or Why Constantinople Fell*, that enjoyed critical acclaim and financial success.

In November 1899 *Ben-Hur* opened on Broadway. The chariot race scene was performed by eight horses pulling two chariots on treadmills installed in the floor. The horses ran at full gallop with background scenery moving behind them. The show ultimately had a twenty-one-year run with six thousand performances seen by twenty million people throughout the western world.

Lew Wallace died quietly at home in 1905.

In 1907 a fifteen-minute "moving picture" of *Ben-Hur* was released. How can you tell the story of this grand opus in fifteen minutes? Wallace's heirs agreed. They sued not so much based upon filming the story without obtaining the rights, but because the film's cheap rendition denigrated the book's creative integrity. The case was finally decided by U.S. Supreme Court Chief Justice Oliver Wendell Holmes in 1911, who ordered the filmmaker to pay $25,000 in damages. It was speculated that the damages exceeded the cost of even producing the film.

MGM obtained the rights in 1925. A silent movie blockbuster was born, receiving critical rave reviews.

Later, in 1959, MGM sought an epic to counter television's severe competition to the motion picture industry. Starring Charlton Heston, *Ben-Hur* won eleven Academy Awards, including Best Picture, Director, Supporting Actor, Musical Score, and Cinematography. Let's say that it swept the Oscars. More recently, the (completely unnecessary) 2016 remake of *Ben-Hur* landed with a thud. It was a colossal flop.

Ben-Hur remained the top-selling book (after the Bible) until Margaret Mitchell's *Gone with the Wind* was released in 1936. After the 1959 film's release, Wallace's book appeared once again on bestseller lists in the 1960s. More than fifty million copies have been sold, and the book has never been out of print since its first printing in 1880.

Chapter 11

1905–1925: Gilded Age Union Wars

The capitalists . . . present a united front in their war upon labor. Through employers' associations, they seek to crush, with brutal force, by the injunctions of the judiciary, and the use of military power, all efforts at resistance.

    Manifesto of the Industrial Workers of the World
    (IWW) Founding Convention, Chicago, Illinois,
    June 27, 1905

On December 30, 1905, former Idaho Governor Frank Steunenberg passed his life insurance physical with flying colors. His newly minted policy was in the pocket of his heavy winter coat pocket as he walked through eight inches of still falling snow. He opened the gate to his home, triggering two nitroglycerin bombs attached to a fishing line. The resulting blast could be heard for miles around.

Steunenberg died within the hour. Responsibility for the murder was immediately focused on the leadership of the Western Federation of Miners (WFM). Law enforcement sought to build a case against the union's leadership based on a retribution motive theory. As governor, Steunenberg had employed a stern collective community punishment in a fantastic chapter of the "Labor Wars" occurring in Northern Idaho in 1899. This historical interlude has come to be known as the Coeur d'Alene Labor Riots, featuring the "Dynamite Express," with the Supreme Court condoning the criminal kidnapping of the most radical labor leader of the time and culminating in a major criminal trial of the century.

Gilded Age greed was tremendous in the mineral resources and mining sector. Vast profits and wealth beckoned. Removing minerals from the ground—a capital-intensive and dangerous enterprise—produced the worst aspects of our capitalist system. Indeed, during this period, mine operators would boast that death and injury were simply part of the mining industry. Miners were required to work twelve to fourteen hours per day in dangerous underground conditions for about $3 a day. The Idaho mining industry experienced intense clashes with union advocates throughout the 1890s and beyond. Brutal tactics were employed by both sides regarding union recognition. The miners sought better pay and working conditions and shorter hours, while the operators sought to increase profits for their shareholders by minimizing costs.

From 1905 to 1920 the Industrial Workers of the World (IWW) organized hundreds of thousands of workers in mines, lumberyards, factories, and farms. It was unquestionably among the most aggressive labor organizations in U.S. history. Strongest in the West, they organized everyone—men and women, African Americans, immigrants—into large industry-wide unions. Big Bill Haywood, secretary-treasurer of the WFM, founder of the IWW, and America's most radical labor boss of the time, was the primary leader of these organizations.

Industrial Workers of the World (IWW) poster condemning child labor, Chicago, c. early twentieth century.

In 1899 the vehemently anti-union Bunker Hill Mining Company, just outside of Coeur d'Alene, was an extremely profitable enterprise. But its miners were earning significantly less than other miners working in surrounding union mines. The company summarily fired anyone suspected of union sympathies and evicted them from company housing. In response, 250 union members hijacked a train, later named the Dynamite Express. While driving that train up the Silver Valley to Bunker Hills' mine, they absconded with three additional box cars to transport almost a thousand union sympathizers to the mine site and, most importantly, four thousand pounds of dynamite.

Many sympathizers on board thought that their role was to picket the mine, unaware of the organizers' ultimate plan of destruction.

By the time the Dynamite Express arrived, most of the workers had fled the mine site. Those remaining were ordered out of the mine. Shots were fired and a few men died. The mine was blown up, and surrounding buildings were burnt to the ground. Wildly cheering crowds greeted the train's return voyage delivering union supporters to their homes.

In response, Governor Steunenberg requested that President William McKinley send federal troops to maintain order as the entire Idaho National Guard was fighting in the Philippines. The army arrived within days. Union supporters were incensed. They had supported Steunenberg's election and saw his actions as a severe betrayal.

Steunenberg declared martial law and ordered warrantless arrests, without evidence, and regardless of profession, of over one thousand Silver Valley men. It was, up until that time, the largest mass arrest in United States history. Most were locked up in horrible, vermin-filled conditions, without adequate protection from the cold nights, for long periods, without trial.

It is fair to say that Steunenberg's actions brought him continued, serious, negative animus from the affected communities.

Harry Orchard had been a WFM bodyguard in Colorado. He later admitted to performing numerous murders, bombings, and other criminal activities on behalf of the union. He was also an informant for the Pinkerton National Detective Agency, at this time the largest private law enforcement organization in the world and regularly utilized by industry against organized labor. Orchard also perpetrated various other swindles and non-violent crimes. After Steunenberg's murder, witnesses recalled seeing Orchard observing the ex-governor's residence from afar using binoculars. A search of Orchard's hotel room found bomb-making materials matching those used in the assassination. He was promptly arrested.

Pinkerton's most famous detective, James McParland, was retained to build the case. His first move: He placed Harry Orchard in solitary confinement for two weeks, without any contact with counsel or family. His food rations were scarce. McParland threatened Orchard that he would hang unless he directly implicated Haywood and two other labor leaders in the Steunenberg assassination plot. Under McParland's skillful, coercive pressure, Orchard supplied the desired, extremely detailed confession, providing prosecutors with the necessary elements of criminal conspiracy. The crime of conspiracy is somewhat vague and elastic. During those times, it was often used by prosecutors (and accepted by courts) as a convenient way to convict members of undesirable groups when trying them for more definitive crimes was too risky.

A **criminal conspiracy** is when two people agree to commit a crime and one of them takes some overt act in furtherance of committing the crime. Both are considered to have committed the crime.

McParland then kidnapped the labor leaders and brought them back to Idaho from Denver, Colorado. He presented the Colorado governor with extradition warrants for Haywood and the other labor leaders as requested by the Idaho prosecutor. They were signed instantly. However, McParland skipped the judicial review requirement, meaning no extradition hearing opportunity was provided whatsoever. Instead, he held the labor leaders incommunicado. No opportunity to bring habeas corpus petitions was available, as the leaders could not notify their attorneys or anyone of their incarceration. McParland spirited them away on a specially arranged, high-speed, nonstop train to Idaho, later dubbed *The Pirate Special*.

The labor leaders brought the kidnapping/habeas corpus issue all the way to the U.S. Supreme Court. The High Court condoned McParland's criminal mode of extradition but allowed it to stand without excusing violated state laws. McParland's kidnapping crime was deemed irrelevant. A single dissenter wrote, "Kidnapping is a crime, pure and simple."[43] To this day, the Supreme Court has yet to invalidate an extradition instituted by a kidnapping and including the denial of any communication with counsel.

No one ever considered charging McParland with this profoundly serious crime.

The worldwide press converged on the trial. The cast of characters and storyline would only drive readership. The defendant, Big Bill Haywood, America's most radical labor leader, was accused of conspiring to murder the former governor. (He was tried first while the other labor leaders sat in jail.) He had a preeminent defense team,

Jury in the Haywood trial.

including Clarence Darrow, who was already famous for representing the United Mine Workers (UMW) before the Anthracite Coal Strike Commission of 1902. William E. Borah, the newly elected Idaho senator and considered to be the best trial lawyer in the state, was on the prosecution team. He had previously obtained guilty verdicts against the Bunker Hill bombers.

James McParland, already a legendary private detective and well known to the public, obtained the confession of the notorious mass murderer Harry Orchard. McParland also employed his standard methods to obtain favorable supporting testimony from another miner, Steve Adams. Orchard had implicated Adams in several murders. Two former union men were set to testify against Haywood. A 1907 newspaper feeding frenzy ensued.

Jury selection took six long weeks. Two hundred forty-nine potential jurors were questioned. Both sides sent scores of investigators into the countryside to obtain information about the prospective jurors. McParland inserted a jury canvasser into the defense team to provide false reports of possible juror preferences. This spy was only exposed late in the jury selection process.

Clarence Darrow performed his usual courtroom magic. While preparing for trial, he was able to convince Adams to recant despite McParland's bullying; instead, Adams testified to McParland's nefarious, coercive methods to obtain confessions. Darrow whittled the case down to the uncorroborated testimony of confessed mass murderer Harry Orchard. Darrow exploited Orchard's extremely violent criminal past, the fact that he had been a paid informant for the mining industry during his bombing and murder spree, and McParland's coercive 'investigative' techniques to extract the damning accusatory confession.

Haywood took the stand for three days in his own defense. He had not been in Idaho for years, denying all of Orchard's allegations, and is credited as eloquently advocating the workingman's cause.

Ruins after the Bunker Hill bombing.

After three months, eighty prosecution witnesses, and one hundred defense witnesses, Darrow presented his closing argument—which went on for eleven hours. The jury of all-male farmers acquitted the radical labor leader after a mere nine hours of deliberation. This highly publicized, long trial gained vast public recognition and sympathy for the horrendous working conditions of western miners.

Group representation issues are heavily influenced by the setting. This tale beautifully illustrates industry and labor conflicts from the 1890s until the Great Depression. With numerous large groups, industry associations, and organized labor in open conflict, it often felt like a true, wartime battlefield. Workers saw the government aligned with reactionary operators, employing selective law enforcement only to aid the titans of industry. The army or national guard was never called upon to protect the working men and women's interests. These forces would intervene, almost always, during strikes and picket lines that involved many participants, creating its own host of group representation issues—particularly, who controls the actions of the individual participants and who is responsible for them.

Strikes and picketing usually involved an element of danger with close contact between union members and strike breakers. It is not hard to imagine, given the large numbers of idle miners and factory workers, frustrated by long hours, low pay, and their employers' disregard for their health and safety, that some would become embroiled in brawls and violations of law. The legal question then arose: Is it fair to hold the unions and their officers responsible for all the acts of union members?

Class actions did not play a role in resolving the question, but previously discussed group representation concepts did. New issues also arose: Do strikes and picketing constitute a conspiracy to interfere with private property rights? Do these actions constitute interference with interstate commerce and hence violate federal anti-trust statutes?

We now arrive at the town of Goldfield, deep in the Nevada desert, about equal distance between Las Vegas and Reno. The 1900 Las Vegas census recorded Goldfield's population as twenty-five, while Reno was a major rail stop and a bustling town of forty-five hundred. In October 1903 gold deposits were discovered in Goldfield, and a town was formally organized—population: thirty-six. The IWW envisioned this remote location as an advantageous place to commence the socialist dream of one big union to organize the entire state.

Goldfield's gold mining caused a population explosion: fifteen thousand souls in 1904; eighteen thousand by 1905; in 1908 a boomtown of over twenty-five thousand. For a brief time, it was Nevada's largest city. By comparison, Reno's 1910 census revealed eleven thousand inhabitants; Las Vegas, eight hundred. This skyrocketing populace still failed to supply the demand for labor. Between 1906 and 1908, the union organized the entire town of Goldfield—all trades, engineers, miners, clerks, waiters, common laborers, newsboys—everyone. The union's dominance was so pervasive that it simply posted the wage rates to be paid, and the maximum number of hours per day and week permissible. The mine owners had little choice but to accept the union's mandated terms.

During the Panic of 1907, a three-week period in mid-October, the NYSE Index fell almost 50 percent, with many banks and businesses filing for bankruptcy. Even though the Goldfield mines were brimming with gold profits, the mine owners altered their manner of payment to miners. Traditionally, miners were paid in cash. Now, the owners adopted a new compensation plan: half the wages in gold, the other half by a cashier's check drawn on the local Goldfield bank. The union miners would have none of this. They demanded cash or guaranteed checks.

The miners went out on strike, unwilling to accept depreciated, or perhaps failing, paper in lieu of money for wages. Picketing was instituted to obtain the strike's goals.

In response, the mine owners sought troops from Nevada Governor John Sparks to 'prevent' violence, claiming, without proof, that property had been dynamited along with other violent felonies. But Sparks had no troops to offer. Nevada simply had no state militia. So Governor Sparks requested President Theodore Roosevelt send federal troops. Roosevelt was mindful of the prior events in Idaho. He did not want the troops to take sides in this "purely industrial dispute," but he sent troops anyway, on a temporary basis, conditional on Nevada organizing a state militia or police force. Those troops were also ordered not to engage unless directly ordered by their superiors in Washington.

Subsequently, the mine owners unilaterally cut the wage rate, further inflaming tensions. If the troops were withdrawn, violence and disorder would certainly ensue. A special session of the Nevada legislature was called, and the Nevada State Police was established.

On March 7, 1908, federal troops withdrew from Goldfield. That same day, the U.S. District Court, in *Goldfield Consol. Mines Co. v. Goldfield Miners' Union No. 220,* issued its group representation ruling.

The main issue: Did the union control the picketers? In the days of Olde England, leaders were deemed responsible for their group. However, the union contended that the subject picketers acted "voluntarily and without preconcert, and without any special direction of the union," and that any miner threatening or intimidating anybody was subject to reprimand and discipline. However, the court found the following evidence very compelling: Members of the union were at the location nearly all the time, day and night, 15 to 150 in number, sometimes as many as 200, apparently directed by "captains." Also, larger numbers would always appear at the time of shift changes.

The district court cited a joint resolution of the Nevada legislature that Goldfield conditions threatened an immediate state of domestic violence. The court also pointed to changes in the Goldfield Miners' Union constitution preamble. It formerly sought "honorable means" to obtain resolution with the mine owners. But in June 1907 that provision was stricken without any language substituted in its place. The court went on to state:

> It is as unreasonable to suppose that these men assembled without design or concert among themselves, and without any direction or understanding with the union or its officers or committees, as it is to suppose that the wheels of a watch get into place by accident.
>
> We may judge the intention and the design of the pickets by their conduct, they have been and are actuated by a common purpose to injure complainant's business by coercing and intimidating its men.[44]

The court issued an injunction against the union and all individually named respondents that prevented them from interfering with the mine owner's business, and the union leaders were deemed responsible for any group or persons violating the injunction. You might notice shades of the "frankpledge" discussed in chapter 2, "1199: Rector Sues His Parishioners."

By 1910 the gold mining operations of Goldfield were in deep decline. Its 1910 census total fell to 4,838, with most of its residents moving on to the next boomtown. In 1913 a flash flood surged through town. After that, about fifteen hundred residents remained. In 1923 a devastating fire followed, emptying the dwindling town further.

The mining companies learned, however, that obtaining an injunction and enforcing it in an economical manner were two entirely different matters. Hence, instead of injunctions, the legal strategy was altered: Go after the union's treasury for damages caused by its members. By targeting the union's coffers, the companies sought to hit the union where it hurt most—in the pocketbook.

This resulted in *two* U.S. Supreme Court cases in a few years between the Coronado Coal Company and District 21 of the United Mine Workers, its officers, various local unions contained within the district, and scores of individuals. The charge: entering a conspiracy to restrain and monopolize interstate commerce, in violation of the Sherman Anti-Trust Act, which included treble damages on awards. Both cases were ultimately decided by Chief Justice William Howard Taft.

Now we turn to yet another American internal 'war': Arkansas' *Sebastian County Union War of 1914*.

In 1914 the western Arkansas coal industry was facing an economic downturn. Depressed industrial conditions, increasingly widespread use of natural gas, overproduction of oil in Texas and Oklahoma, a depressed cotton industry, and mild winters were the leading causes. The UMW was weak in the South except for Arkansas. In 1903 every miner in the state was a union member, and every mine operated on a "closed shop" basis.

Journey through our visual interpretation of history, where heroes, villains, and visionaries shaped our laws, as each chapter reveals the collective struggle for fairness carried forward from past courage into our shared future.

A symbolic reflection on the fragile weight of power, where crowns were won through blood, conflict, and claim, and the struggle for rightful rule shaped early justice echoing through centuries into the laws we inherit.

A stark depiction of defiance met with ruthless force, where a lone cleric's stand against royal power revealed the peril of confronting unchecked authority and shaped the centuries-long fight for lawful justice.

A weathered emblem of an empire pushed to its breaking point, where conflict and revolt reshaped nations, and the struggle for representation rose from the ashes to redefine justice far beyond the reach of kings.

The 1899 Bunker Hill Mine explosion accentuated the deep tensions in the western mining industry between labor and industry during this period, leading to court cases about collective responsibility when pursuing justice.

An artist's depiction of John Wesley and Abraham Lincoln framed within the Methodist tradition that has guided generations, but culminating in splitting the faith between north and south over slavery.

Jersey and Guernsey islanders bringing their grievances before a local church rector.

The burning of the British schooner Gaspee, the 1772 Rhode Island attack that marked the first organized colonial strike against the Crown's authority.

The Second Great Awakening in the 1840s, a period of intense religious revival in America.

General Lew Wallace, the author of Ben Hur, at work, creating numerous legacies impacting the administration of justice in America.

Honoring the courage and legacy of the plaintiff families in Brown v. Board of Education, which challenged segregation and reshaped American jurisprudence regarding equality under the law.

General Dwight D. Eisenhower reviewing intelligence derived from the newly minted Colossus II computer, demonstrating the vital role early codebreaking technology played in defeating the Nazis.

Bristol's privateering era; where commerce, naval power, and sanctioned piracy intersected in a system of profit, risk, and royal authority.

We always head into the future from the learning and experience of the past.

—Troy Ian Hoffman

A **closed shop** is a collective bargaining contract term. The employer agrees that only union members will be hired and remain employed.

Franklin Bache owned many of Sebastian County's coal mines. He was openly hostile to organized labor and collective bargaining. To avoid contractual obligations to the miners under Arkansas law, he transferred ownership of operations to an out-of-state corporate shell. Bache then hired highly armed strike breakers. Union officials publicly cautioned against the use of violence. A group of union men loosened the caps on the mine's boilers, allowing the steam to escape and extinguishing the fires for its generators. There was little damage, but the mines could not operate as the water pumps were turned off. The mines quickly filled with water. Bache obtained a temporary restraining order against the union, which only caused other miners in Bache's control to walk out.

Bache then filed another lawsuit, this time claiming damages under a conspiracy theory. Besides the alleged property damage and his cost of paying fifty federal marshals to protect the property, he even sought reimbursement for costs related to summarily evicting union sympathizers from company-owned property.

Hence, the question arose: Can a union, an unincorporated association, be sued as if it were a corporation, with a resulting judgment against the union's vast treasury, or did its members have to be sued individually? In this case, the union, the unincorporated association, had four hundred thousand members, a wide array of officers, a sophisticated organizational structure, and abundant strike funds.

An **unincorporated association** is a voluntary collection of individuals that traditionally could not sue or be sued in its own name. The association must operate through its members or a board acting as trustees.

The Arkansas federal district court trial resulted in a verdict of $200,000 for the plaintiffs, trebled by the court pursuant to anti-trust laws, counsel fees of $25,000, and $120,600 in interest. It came to almost $850,000 in total.

When this first case reached the High Court, Chief Justice William Howard Taft's opinion in *United Mine Workers of America v. Coronado Coal Co.* (1922) found little evidence of a union conspiracy to restrict the movement of non-union coal to markets outside of Arkansas, a required prerequisite for a Sherman Anti-Trust Act violation. However, Chief Taft broadened group representation jurisprudence in America. The case established a federal precedent that unincorporated unions could be party to a civil suit and, as a 'group,' responsible for the actions of its members. Hence, if evidence existed to prove a conspiracy, then union funds were subject to seizure in suits for torts committed by the union during a strike. A powerful litigation weapon indeed.

Taft's opinion cited Justice Story's *Equity Pleading* treatise: "More than this, equitable procedure adapting itself to modern needs has grown to recognize the need of representation by one person of many, too numerous to sue or to be sued."

Taft discussed the union's operations:

> Extensive financial business is carried on, money is borrowed, notes are given to banks, and in every way the union acts as a business

entity, distinct from its members. No organized corporation has greater unity of action, and in none is more power centered in the governing executive bodies.

But from an evidentiary perspective, Chief Taft wrote that:

[T]here is nothing to show that the International Board ever authorized it, took any part in preparation for it or in its maintenance. Nor did they or their organization ratify it by paying any of the expenses. It came exactly within the definition of a local strike in the constitutions of both the national and the district organizations.[45]

The company lost simply because it lacked evidence that the UMW International was involved in the strike activity. The chief implied that if such evidence were obtained, the result would be different. So the company searched for new evidence and found a new witness.

James K. McNamara was a union leader during the 1914 labor conflict. He served as secretary for a local union. McNamara claimed that he met with District President Pete Stewart and the UMW President John P. White to discuss stopping Coronado "scab dug" coal from reaching the market—a deliberate plot to impede interstate commerce. McNamara testified that White provided instructions to inform membership of the plans. He further swore that Stewart offered firearms to mine families to restrict non-union coal movement.

In the second trial, the plaintiffs were awarded $625,000, which included the anti-trust treble damages and attorney fees. When this case, *Coronado Coal Co. v. United Mine Workers of America* (1925), reached the Supreme Court, they unanimously reversed their 1922 decision. Commentators contend that the ruling blurred the legal standing of strikes interfering with goods entering interstate commerce.

Chief Taft's opinion in favor of the company was limited to the local union district, not the national UMW. The court's opinion broadly declared that labor unions possessed an unquestioned right of peaceful persuasion, but it limited picketing to a single person at each gate, seemingly impractical for mines or plants employing hundreds, and muddling the law regarding serious social and economic conflict.

After two trips to the Supreme Court, the union was able to settle the case for a mere $27,500. But the case adversely obstructed the labor movement itself. New questions were raised about the legality of strikes affecting interstate trade. The UMW in Arkansas was negatively impacted, as the ruling caused the state's coal mines to become predominately non-union.

Organized labor found some relief from the New Deal Congress. The Norris-La Guardia Act of 1932 declared that labor unions were not combinations or conspiracies restraining trade and removed injunctions against union organizing activities from management's legal arsenal. The National Labor Relations Act (NLRA) of 1935, also called the Wagner Act, went further, by initiating federal oversight of employer interference with unions' organizational efforts and protecting collective bargaining rights. The National Labor Relations Board has administrative oversight of these incredibly significant group representation issues.

UMW membership rose to over six hundred thousand during the 1930s and '40s. Today there are only about twenty-five thousand active union miners. Coal is no longer king. Arkansas only retains an exceedingly small coal mining industry, with no active UMW members.

Goldfield, Nevada, the one-time boom town, has less than two hundred residents today. The hometown's current primary enterprise: the town itself. It is one of the largest, best preserved ghost towns in America.

Big Bill Haywood opposed U.S. involvement in World War I. He and other labor leaders were charged with violating espionage and sedition acts by calling for wartime strikes. All were convicted.

When the Supreme Court rejected his final appeal in 1921, Haywood jumped bail and fled to the Soviet Union.

Vladimir Lenin ensured that Haywood was respected within his new country. However, he was marginalized when Joseph Stalin ascended to power. After Haywood's death in Moscow in 1928, half of his ashes were buried in the Kremlin Wall near famed American journalist and communist activist John Reed, the only other American so interred. The other half of his ashes is buried by the Haymarket Martyrs' Monument in Chicago.

Chapter 12

1936: The Birth of Grandfather 23

Take me out to the ball game,
Take me out with the crowd;
Buy me some peanuts and Cracker Jacks,
I don't care if I never get back.
Let me root, root, root
For the home team,
If they don't win it's a shame.
For it's one, two, three strikes you're out,
At the old ball game.
—*Jack Norworth and Albert Von Tilzer,*
"Take Me Out to the Ball Game," 1908

April 10, 1910. Opening Day for baseball at National's Park in Washington, D.C. Walter Johnson, in his fourth season, is the starting pitcher for the Washington club. The special feeling of opening day had some extra excitement for the hometown crowd: President William Howard Taft was in attendance. Unbeknownst to the fans (and the president), Taft started two great American traditions that day. He was the first president to throw out the ceremonial first pitch. In those days, the act was performed from the stands, unchanged until Ronald Reagan took the mound.

Then, in the historic seventh inning, President Taft needed to stand up and stretch. In respect, and believing that the president was preparing to leave, the entire crowd also stood up. When Taft didn't leave, they continued standing until the president sat down, providing the presidential seal of approval to the previously casual seventh inning stretch. Another great baseball tradition was born.

Taft had no idea of the lasting impact that his 'stretch' that day would have on America. A leader's simple act with the group following—Taft unknowingly set a tradition lasting now for over one hundred years.

No one sang "Take Me Out to the Ballgame," though. That tradition did not start until the 1934 World Series. However, the fans did get to see Walter Johnson strike out nine batters and pitch a one-hit shutout. That performance added to the 110 shutouts that Johnson would ultimately throw in his career, still remaining a major league record to this day. Of course, how could President Taft, or anyone, know that Johnson would ultimately become a star for the ages?

Taft was appointed Supreme Court chief justice by President Warren Harding, making him the only person ever to hold both that post and the presidency. Taft later played an important, and equally unwitting, role in the birth of the modern class action. That story takes a bit more development because, as we know, the law is usually more complicated than three strikes and you're out.

Once upon a time, there were no Federal Rules of Civil Procedure. Before the mid-1930s, federal courts were guided by the *conformity principle*: federal practice followed state procedural rules of the location of each U.S. district court. Obviously, this created disparities in procedural rulings across federal districts. Since the passage of the 1792 Process Act, Congress required circuit and district courts to follow the civil procedures of the states in which they were domiciled. John Marshall, the second Supreme Court chief justice, described in an 1825 opinion, "A judicial system was to be prepared, not for a consolidated people, but for distinct societies, already possessing distinct systems." Translation: Each state was unique, and we should not try to superimpose the federal government on each state's individuality.

But different procedural rules in each federal district court made things complicated. Congress had empowered the Supreme Court to establish rules for equity procedure in the federal courts. Initial Equity Rules were created in 1822. Later, in 1842, Equity Rule 47 was established to deal generally with "necessary party" issues. Rule 48 dealt with situations "[w]here the parties on either side are very numerous . . . [that] the decree shall be without prejudice to the rights and claims of all the absent parties." Hence, no class actions existed in our modern understanding of this concept, as a "representative" could not stand in for a "class."

As shown in the 1854 ruling of *Smith v. Swormstedt*, absentees could be bound in a "representative" suit. This was an important pillar of class action law in America. The 1842 Equity Rules that the very same court had proclaimed a scant twelve years earlier were essentially ignored. From 1854 until 1912, when the Equity Rules were revised, Rule 48 and *Swormstedt* coexisted in quiet incongruity.

In the Conformity Act of 1872, Congress reaffirmed its commitment to the use of state procedures in federal courts. True conformity between federal trial courts remained elusive. Beginning in the late 1880s, prominent lawyers and the newly formed American Bar Association, founded in 1878, began calling for replacing inconsistent conformity with federal court uniformity. It seems that Sir Francis Bacon and Justice Joseph Story were their coaches and trainers.

President William Howard Taft, in his 1910 annual message to Congress, proposed that the Supreme Court be provided the authority to draft rules of civil procedure for federal courts. Supporters argued that the rules devised by the Supreme Court were preferable to those made by the states. The federal judiciary had more expertise and flexibility to respond to necessary changes and would create simpler rules. State court lawyers, it was argued, wouldn't feel challenged by new, simple federal rules.

Do I hear some attorneys chuckling over that claim?

1912 was a big year: the *Titanic* sank, Fenway Park opened, Paramount Pictures was founded, the Japanese gifted three thousand cherry trees to be planted in Washington, D.C., and the first parachute jump occurred. In November of that year, Woodrow Wilson won the election for the presidency, defeating incumbent President William Howard Taft and former President Theodore Roosevelt. Most importantly for us, the newly revised Federal Equity Rules became effective.

New class action Rule 38 replaced former Rule 48. It stated, "When the question is one of common or general interest to many persons constituting a class so numerous as to make it impracticable to bring them all before the court, one or more may sue or defend for the whole." The only significant change from the old Rule was that the absentees' rights reservation was removed. *Swormstedt* and the Equity Rules were now congruous. Some sense of order was emerging.

Discussion persisted as to whether the Supreme Court had the capacity to study and write new rules in addition to managing its growing caseload, and to even respond to practicing lawyers' concerns. The High Court needed assistance. It was also argued that Supreme Court justices were too far removed from ordinary litigants and would be unresponsive to complaints about the operation of the rules. If litigants had a problem with state rules, they could petition their legislatures; a code written by Congress would give people a political channel in which to raise concerns.

A uniform federal rules bill failed to pass in the Senate throughout the 1910s and 1920s, even with the vocal support of

Chief Justice Taft. In 1922 Taft's lobbying resulted in the creation of the Conference of Senior Circuit Judges—later renamed the Judicial Conference of the United States—a foundational institution in the formation of our modern class action rules, Federal Rules of Civil Procedure Rule 23.

President Franklin Delano Roosevelt's 1930s New Deal increased the federal role in many areas of American life. Concern existed that this expanded role was too similar to the rising tide of worldwide fascism, the existential battle over the scope of the national administrative state. The Supreme Court overturned many of FDR's programs.

In 1934 FDR's attorney general, Homer Cummings, recognizing that the federal legal system faced serious challenges, lobbied strongly for a uniform federal procedure bill to bring order and efficiency to federal courts. A new, consistent federal practice for all courts would bring harmony to the expanding federal role and its programs. Consistency throughout the federal courts was the goal. Marshall's concept of "distinct societies" for each state . . . ancient history.

In 1934, the same year Walt Disney started working on his first feature-length film *Snow White and the Seven Dwarfs*, the U.S. Congress passed The Rules Enabling Act. It granted the judicial branch, via the Judicial Conference of the United States, the authority to promulgate the Federal Rules of Civil Procedure so that a single, consistent body of rules for all civil actions would be used in federal court. Congress finally recognized the inherent problem of different federal districts utilizing each state's differing procedural rules while administering federal lawsuits. It only took fifty years from the time that leading bar members commenced the discussion.

Under the statute, the new rules of civil procedure would become active if not rejected by Congress within sixty days of their adoption by the Supreme Court. This addressed the concerns of those fearing the lack of a legislative or political mechanism for citizen or state lawyers' input.

An important clause of the Rules Enabling Act (28 USC § 2072(b)) for our discussion states:

> Such rules shall not abridge, enlarge or modify any substantive right. All laws in conflict with such rules shall be of no further force or effect after such rules have taken effect.

In May 1935 the Supreme Court went full throttle, authorizing the drafting of new rules for a united system of law and equity. U.S. Supreme Court Justice Charles Evans Hughes, in his annual address to the American Law Institute, said, "After careful consideration . . . the Court has decided not to prepare rules limited to common law cases but to proceed with the preparation of a unified system of rules for cases in equity and actions at law, so as to secure one form of civil action and procedure for both, so far as this may be done without the violation of any substantive right."[46]

This is quite a trick, changing procedural rules without altering any substantive law. Consider, for instance, the statute of limitations requiring plaintiffs to file their lawsuits within a certain time frame, or their cause is forever barred. At some point, cases, facts, memories, and witnesses become too distant to be fair to defendants. Who wants to be served with a lawsuit five years after the incident or dispute? But what about the plaintiff filing an amended or supplemental pleading that speaks to their earlier filing? The rules state that it "relates back," meaning procedurally the new filing is deemed to have been filed on the old date to preserve the substantive right. That is deemed *procedural* even though it certainly seems to change a *substantive* right.

Food for thought, but I will go no further. I'm just accenting the contours of the drafters' playing field. They can't outwardly alter substantive law, or they'd violate The Rules Enabling Act. Drafting these rules was tricky business.

The Rules Enabling Act authorizes the Supreme Court to appoint an advisory committee. The nation's leading lawyers and legal scholars assembled, relying on input from lawyers in each federal district. This led to the creation of a more powerful Judicial Conference. Supreme Court Chief Justice Taft assembled the team, sitting on the metaphorical bench, preparing, and training for this new, most important opening day.

The final adoption of the Federal Rules of Civil Procedure greatly altered practice in the federal courts. The Federal Rules are generally credited as leading to simplified pleading, broad discovery, and more judicial discretion.

In 1937 Amelia Earhart attempted the first circumnavigation of the globe, only to become forever lost. Joe Louis won his dramatic heavyweight title fight, and General Motors finally recognized the United Auto Workers. The Spanish Civil War became the practice grounds for World War II. The opening of the Golden Gate Bridge gave America a new spirit of pride, and Walt Disney premiered *Snow White and the Seven Dwarfs*, the first feature-length animated film. 1937 also saw the creation of the Federal Rules of Civil Procedure Rule 23 governing class actions. But the Judicial Conference drafters knew a difficult task lay ahead. Famed legal scholar, Yale Law Professor James William Moore, holding the post of research assistant to the reporter for the Advisory Committee on Rules for Civil Procedure (and soon-to-be author of a thirty-one-volume treatise on civil procedure), wrote in an early 1937 law review article:

> The law on class actions is inextricably bound up with jurisdiction, and the binding effect of the judgment, and because of these complexities is in a confused state. A real service would be rendered the profession if a rule were promulgated which was really informative. It is difficult, however, to appraise the various problems involved and state a technically sound and thoroughly workable rule. Danger lies in the rigidity of a detailed rule.[47]

Or more simply, this stuff is quite complex, so we need simple rules.

But throughout history, group litigation or class actions have always been designed to fit the issues of the times. As we have already seen from the previous stories, their flexibility must be retained as strict rules are unmanageable when dealing with numerous parties. The soon-to-be-born FRCP 23 was written by a judicial committee, not developed by case law over time. The 1937 rule had no choice but to comport with contemporary state and federal laws that created rights applicable to "classes" of litigants' standard at that time, such as association members, shareholders, or creditors, but also with appreciation that sacrificing the individual rights of putative class members violated tradition. By creating class definitions by the character of the right sought to be applied, the initial FRCP 23(b) relied upon pre-determined relationships, akin to Sir Edward Coke's ruling in the *Case of Sutton's Hospital* (chapter 4).

The committee was charged with simplifying and restraining the complexity—not only by statute (to avoid changing substantive law) but also limited by the scant history of group litigation that came before. They had no crystal ball to foresee the future.

The original FRCP 23(b)(1)-(3) had two initial prerequisites that remain within the statute today:

1. numerosity: the impracticability to litigate claims individually
2. adequacy of representation: class members sufficiently representing the applicable interests of the entire class

Lawyer competence was not considered at that time. Once these two requirements were met, a class action could proceed if it fell into one of three categories: true, hybrid, or spurious.

Spurious was an odd word choice for a case category. The word originates from the Latin *spurius*, meaning false. But in sixteenth-century England, it was derogatorily used to describe a person born out of wedlock. In Roman times, though it did mean an illegitimate offspring, it wasn't used disparagingly. Yet spurious is the title the learned drafters named that form of class action.

"Plaintiff Pete, we have filed and served your spurious class action." I am not sure that it elicits Pete's confidence when the lawyer calls his lawsuit *spurious*.

The *hybrid* and *spurious* categories were less straightforward. They were similar, as they invited parties to intervene into the lawsuit (please come and participate). Today the term is *opt-in*, meaning you have a choice to be part of the class action or not.

A *hybrid* judgment was only conclusive and binding on absent parties with respect to claims affecting the contested property or funds at issue, such as in a receivership or stockholder case.

The *spurious* category was more confusing, as it was created essentially to manipulate a jurisdictional ambiguity by allowing a party to intervene regardless of state citizenship or claim amount. This invited intervenors without requiring an independent basis of federal jurisdiction. Consider this akin to present-day defendants welcoming, or even seeking to expand, a class action settlement to permit finality from ever repeating similar lawsuits. However, it didn't adjudicate the rights or liabilities of non-parties.

As with many things that are untrue—it didn't work out so well. Nobody liked it very much due to the gaping hole of failing to address non-parties. Then again, there were few cases about which to be overly concerned.

While Professor Moore sought simplicity, the three FRCP 23 categories provoked uncertainty. They offered inventive courts and counsel significant flexibility to interpret the rule liberally and thus enlarge their reach. Placing a lawsuit within one of the three categories was difficult and created new legal disputes. Once a class action was characterized, the judgment's binding effect opened the doors to repeated post judgment challenges. Courts avoided the thorny issues of class categories. Adequacy of notice issues were left until it was required to make a determination, later on, of a prior judgment's effect on absent class members.

Due process and notice issues were not addressed in the original 1937 rule. In the 1937 version of FRCP 23, *hybrid* or *spurious* class actions had nary a discussion of notice requirements considered critical today. The rule's failure to require notice became obvious as courts faced due process case law considerations, particularly in *Mullane v. Hanover Bank*, discussed in the next chapter. From my perch, this is a wide, gaping hole. But more than eighty years have passed since those fine minds of yesteryear addressed these issues.

The *spurious* rule was ultimately deemed defective, as anything false is apt to be, and it was essentially ignored soon after its passage. There was not another substantive change until the 1966 FRCP Rule 23 changes I'll discuss in chapter 16, "1966: The Year Everything Changed." These mostly govern federal class actions to this day. But, like many things, we need to try and test early models until they can become more perfect.

The next chapters lead us through thirty years of a changing ballgame involving racial discrimination, providing notice in a more complicated world, and finality of judgment issues, toward the ultimate need to revisit the federal class action rules. Even though the past is never finished, we always head into the future by learning the historical experiences that came before us.

Chapter 13

1940–1950: Due Process Trumps Racially Restrictive Covenants

I want you to believe me when I tell you that race prejudice simply doesn't enter into it. It is a matter of the people of Clybourne Park believing, rightly or wrongly, as I say, that for the happiness of all concerned that our Negro families are happier when they live in their own communities.

—Lorraine Hansberry, A Raisin in the Sun,
Act II, scene iii, 1959

In 1877, at the end of the Civil War Reconstruction Era, federal troops left the South. Jim Crow state laws were instituted, systematically suppressing African American voting, enforcing segregation of everything from schools and transportation to lunch counters and drinking fountains, and mandating inferior, underfunded public facilities. These policies were supported by mob violence and thousands of lynchings.

Starting around 1910, with no hope for social or economic opportunity, Blacks fled the Jim Crow South. Northern jobs in meatpacking plants, steel mills, railroads, and the rising auto industry beckoned. These sectors sent labor agents south to recruit workers by offering free transportation and low-cost housing, along with other incentives.

Between 1910 and 1970, more than five million African Americans left the South for Northern cities. It was the largest migration of humans within the same country in the history of mankind that was not caused by threats of death from the hostilities of war or starvation. It eclipsed the historic immigrant waves of Italians, Poles, Irish, and Jews to America. Individually, none of these groups surpassed five million.

Prior to 1910 more than 90 percent of former slaves were living in the South. By 1960 slightly more than 50 percent remained. The First Great Migration began with an exodus of 1.6 million people, fueled by armament industries building for World War I. It lasted until 1940. The Second Great Migration, lasting from 1940 to 1970, forever changed the socioeconomic and demographic balances of many Northern urban areas. For the purposes of our story, these changes spurred many "race relations" cases, as they were called in those days.

Carl A. Hansberry, the plaintiff in *Hansberry v. Lee*, was born in 1895 in Gloster, Mississippi, just north of the Louisiana panhandle border. This was indisputably the Deep South. The population of Gloster was approximately fifteen hundred. The 1900 and 1920 censuses for Gloster revealed a drop of 27 percent in the small town's population. Hansberry was one of those departees, moving to Chicago during the First Great Migration.

By 1900 Chicago had 30,000 Black residents. By 1934 there were 236,000 living mostly in the "Black Belt": two long, narrow corridors running from the city's center, one running south, the other west. Chicago was a highly segregated city. 1918 saw the end of World War

Carl Hansberry, Chicago businessman and civil rights activist, c. 1930s.

I. White men returning home found their jobs taken by Black men willing to work for lower pay. In 1919, as tensions flared in Chicago, major rioting ensued, with thirty-eight dead and more than five hundred injured. Untold Black properties were destroyed, leaving thousands homeless.

During this period, similar orchestrated attacks on African American communities occurred in Northern and Midwestern cities. Indeed, in 1967 racial tensions still ran high in Chicago. During a housing discrimination march through Chicago, Dr. Martin Luther King, Jr., reported that his reception by Whites was worse than any treatment he had ever received in the South. Of all his marches, he was most afraid in Chicago.

The Windy City is still considered the most segregated city in America.

In response to mass Black migration to Northern cities, Whites started a program of racially restrictive covenants in real estate deeds. Restrictive covenants were formal agreements, neighbors pledging not to sell or rent homes to Blacks and other minorities. These agreements, however, didn't just apply to the signatories; they were registered with county records of land ownership. This was a legal agreement that flowed with the land, like commitments made when purchasing a condominium today. Courts consistently honored these agreements. Purchasers of property containing these covenants were required to honor them. The use of racially restrictive covenants exploded. Migrating Blacks traded the South's Jim Crow for the North's segregation.

In 1926 the Supreme Court's *Corrigan v. Buckley* decision upheld the usage of racially restrictive covenants. The Chicago Real Estate Board promptly instituted a program to 'protect' neighborhoods utilizing these covenants. The board actively visited chambers of commerce and property owners' associations, YMCAs, churches, and women's clubs, PTAs, and Kiwanis clubs. Segregationist Chicago boasted that 80 percent of the city used racially restrictive covenants. If you were one-eighth Negro, using the term of the day, then the covenant applied, the same percentile used in Nazi Germany to determine if a person was Jewish.

All the while, Black demand for housing continued to increase along with a depressed market for White housing. The system of segregation created by racially restrictive covenants began breaking down in the 1930s due to the growth of Chicago's Black population and the economics of the Depression.

Plaintiff Carl Hansberry found part of his American dream in Chicago. He was a deputy U.S. marshal, a successful businessman and real estate agent, an unsuccessful Republican candidate for Congress, and a well-known Black civil rights activist. He founded the

Lake Street Bank, one of Chicago's first Black-owned financial institutions. His wife, schoolteacher Nannie Louise Perry, was a ward committeewoman and socialite, hosting parties with luminaries such as Joe Louis, Langston Hughes, and Paul Robeson.

In *Hansberry v. Lee* Carl Hansberry was far from a "stand in" civil rights plaintiff. He intentionally bought a house in a White neighborhood that fell under the racial covenant, moving his family with the objective of challenging the segregationist character of South Chicago. He told *The Defender*, a well-respected Black Chicago newspaper, that he did so with "the purpose of trying to have the theory of restrictive covenants once and for all abolished or declared as against the public policy of the state and nation." *The Defender* called him "a Real Race Man"—someone deeply committed to the struggle for equal rights.

Simple economics also played a role in the transaction. Hansberry was the only person interested in buying the house, but the transaction was not straightforward. The property had to be acquired before the White neighbors learned that a Black family was moving in. A clandestine deal was required in anticipation of neighborhood hostility to Black people. Such was life for African Americans in 1937.

The covenant-covered property was conveyed to a third party and the title then transferred to a bank. Immediately thereafter, a dummy corporation (a business organized as a false front to hide the true owner) purchased the property for Hansberry, using a Black-owned insurance company as the trustee on the note and Hansberry as the guarantor. Once these rapid transactions were completed, Mr. Hansberry and his family moved into their newly acquired South Chicago residence.

A family moving into a new home is usually reason to rejoice. But as word spread, the Hansberry family was besieged by howling mobs. A brick thrown through the residence's window "almost took the life of the then eight-year-old signer of this letter," Carl's daughter, Lorraine Hansberry, later wrote. She recalled, "My memories of this 'correct' way of fighting white supremacy in America include being spat at, cursed and pummeled in the daily trek to and from school." Sadly, these occurrences still occur too frequently to this day.

And now, the lawsuits.

CASE #1: *BURKE V. KLEIMAN*

Burke v. Kleiman was a 1934 Illinois state court case involving the same racially restrictive covenant that Hansberry ultimately challenged. Under the terms of the covenant, it only took effect if signed by 95 percent of the designated area residents. Olive Burke was a passionate defender of these covenants. Indeed, it was a family affair, as her husband, James, was then serving on the Property Owners Association. In this case, Olive initiated a state court injunction and conspiracy action to enjoin other property owners from violating the covenant. She filed on behalf of herself and the other property owners, a group representation action. The defendants were property owners renting apartment units to Black families.

The named defendants entered a stipulation that 95 percent of the owners had signed the covenant. A stipulation in court is a formal agreement between those parties regarding certain facts. They are often utilized to save court time on undisputed matters. Because of the stipulation, Olive Burke was not required to prove that 95 percent agreed to and signed onto the covenant. She contended that the restrictions did not violate the U.S. Constitution. No constitutional counter arguments were raised by the defendants. No objection as to whether Burke was a valid representative of the property owners was mentioned either. Defendants' quarrel was limited to Burke waiting too long in moving for her injunction, and that the covenant was no longer material as the character of the neighborhood had already changed. Not the most passionate defense.

The trial court dutifully issued the requested injunction in a case lacking a true adversarial nature. The Illinois Supreme Court affirmed the lower court's ruling.

During this time, more Northern White attitudes about race were evolving in appreciation of the injustice of the racially restrictive covenants. Among them, James Burke, experiencing a change of heart about the propriety of the covenant program, resigned from the presidency of the Property Owners Association.

CASE #2: *LEE V. HANSBERRY*

Lee v. Hansberry was initially commenced in 1937 as an Illinois state court action brought by Anna Lee and other area residents who were party to the restrictive covenant. They sought to enforce the covenant and reverse the Hansberry real estate purchase. Besides defendant Hansberry, James Burke, Olive's husband in the first case, was also a defendant in this action. He sold the subject property to Hansberry, albeit indirectly, in breach of the covenant. Burke's actions violated the court's earlier judgment previously obtained by his wife. But he was also a source of great knowledge regarding the insider facts of the previous case that would aid Hansberry's cause.

Defendant Hansberry asserted that the required 95 percent of property owners never actually signed the covenant; the *Burke v. Kleiman* defendants only signed a stipulation that they had done so. The trial court in this second case accepted the fact that the association executive secretary knew that 95 percent of the property owners had not signed the covenant agreement, presumably from insider knowledge provided by James Burke. In fact, the trial court found that only 54 percent of the area's property holders had signed the accord, finding the previous suit collusive. However, the Illinois trial court sustained the covenant anyway, determining that the previous lawsuit was a class suit and hence binding on all property owners and their successors, even though the key factual issue—whether the covenant was valid—was never litigated in the prior case.

The Illinois Supreme Court affirmed the trial court's ruling. The court stated, "it thus appears that *Burke v. Kleiman* was a class or representative suit."[48]

The Illinois Supreme Court found that while the stipulation in the earlier suit was untrue, it was not collusive. The issues presented regarding the "execution and validity of the restrictive agreement are *res judicata*," meaning the decision was final and could not be adjudicated.

The dissent was deeply concerned that

> The undisputed fact is that by means of fraud and collusion between total strangers an agreement which is void on its face has been imposed upon some ten million dollars worth of the property of five hundred other parties who were never in court, who never had notice of any law suit, who were never by name or as unknown owners made parties to any law suit, and who have never been accorded any process whatever, either due or otherwise.

The dissent wisely prognosticated:

> [I]t seems clear to me that a class suit cannot properly be entertained except in that very limited field of cases where the parties have not only a common and general interest among themselves but also an identical right to be protected in a single and undivided *res*.
>
> Due process most certainly requires notice and an opportunity to be heard, and no case has come to my attention where the court has failed to make absolutely certain, in advance, that the parties to represent a class must be selected with such care and

have such personal interest in the litigation as to guarantee that the rights of all will be fully protected.[49]

Mr. Hansberry headed to the U.S. Supreme Court. As Hansberry was the petitioner, the case was now entitled *Hansberry v. Lee*.

In this 1940 case, the High Court considered it their "duty" to examine whether the plaintiff was afforded notice and opportunity to be heard consistent with the due process clause of the U.S. Constitution, while acknowledging the *Smith v. Swormstedt* rule "there is a recognized exception that, to an extent not precisely defined by judicial opinion, the judgment in a 'class' or 'representative' suit, to which some members of the class are parties, may bind members of the class or those represented who were not made parties to it."

The *Hansberry* court ruled that the *Burke v. Kleiman* judgment could not apply to non-parties if their interests were not adequately represented. The court held, "[w]e decide only that the procedure and the course of litigation sustained here by the plea of *res judicata* do not satisfy these requirements." The court discussed the jurisprudential principle that people cannot be bound by a judgment when they were never designated as a party or served with the complaint. The court also reasoned that some signers or successors to the restrictive covenant may not seek or wish its enforcement and hence cannot be in the same 'class' as those seeking to have it enforced. Olive Burke did not genuinely represent the interests of all the property owners. Kleiman never represented the interests of those negatively impacted by the covenant.

The High Court also found that the pleadings and court ruling of the prior case did not treat those defendants as representing others. Hence, without any representation in the initial 'class suit' in Illinois state court, the prior decree enforcing the racially restrictive covenant simply could not be enforced against Mr. Hansberry. Indeed, the prior case involved property owners renting rooms to Blacks, while

Mr. Hansberry was purchasing the home as his family residence. The court, appreciating that "class actions" were a just-budding litigation device requiring better judicial guidance and clarity, further acknowledged that the "doctrine of representation of absent parties in a class suit has not hitherto been thought to go so far."

The Court understood that the legal landscape was changing. Class action law was bound to expand in scope. But opportunities for fraudulent, collusive behavior that sacrificed the rights of absent, unrepresented parties was at least addressed, serving as a foundational principle for our present FRCP Rule 23. Fully tackling "adequacy of representation" class action criteria within the federal rules was still another twenty-five years away, as we'll see in chapter 16, "1966: The Year Everything Changed."

Mr. Hansberry won—but not on the terms he wished as a "Real Race Man." The court avoided Hansberry's discrimination reality on the ground and instead wrote an abstract essay about due process in class actions. While a critical foundation for class action law, the court was not ready to deal with racial and constitutional issues. Instead, it categorized the case as concerning the constitutional parameters of class action notice and representation.

Significantly, support or discussion regarding then-recently formulated Rule 23 was completely absent from the opinion. But consider the procedural morass. The underlying actions were in state court under Illinois' court rules. The state court opinion expressed doubt whether the underlying first case actually *was* a class action, or if it just *seemed* to be. No modern-day court or litigator would ever be similarly uncertain.

The Supreme Court did, however, lay down an important marker in due process law—*res judicata* cannot bind a plaintiff whose interests were not represented in an earlier civil action. Ten years later, in its 1950 seminal ruling in *Mullane v. Central Hanover Bank*, the High

Court issued an even more important ruling impacting the future FRCP Rule 23, involving due process notice in pending class actions.

Before and during the mid-1930s, corporate trustees administering an increasing number of small trust estates faced a problem. Standard doctrine was that a trustee could not allow trust assets from one trust to be commingled with assets from other trusts. But how could the trustee then adequately protect small trusts with diversified investments and avoid high administrative expenses and thereby obtain rates of return comparable to large trusts? Often trust companies were forced to take a loss when administering small trusts. To fix this problem, several states, including New York, passed laws permitting the pooling of small trusts into a larger common fund then administered by a corporate fiduciary.

In *Mullane* the bank petitioned the local court to settle the first accounting as common trustee. The New York court, cognizant that some beneficiaries did not receive adequate notice of their legal rights, appointed Kenneth Mullane as special guardian and attorney for all parties, known or unknown, who possessed any interest in the fund's income. This procedure was common so that courts could ensure beneficiaries were protected. The New York law's notice provision permitted newspaper publication of the action without even naming the beneficiaries, the very parties naturally interested in the proceeding. At the time of the original investment, the bank sent notice via mail, pursuant to New York law, that each participant was entitled to their share of income and about the judicial settlement process.

The newspaper notices only included the name of the trust, the estates within the trust, and the date it was established. No requirement existed that the beneficiary's names be included. Mullane objected to the New York statute's notice provision, contending that it did not provide adequate due process rights. The trial court disagreed, accepting the trustee's accounting and terminating any beneficiary rights that may have existed against the bank for trust mismanagement.

Mullane then appealed to both of New York's higher courts. The appeals failed. So, like Mr. Hansberry, he went off to the Supreme Court and found some due process success in the federal judiciary that had been denied to him in state court.

The High Court found that constructive service via newspaper publication was unreliable to provide notice, as newspapers have limited circulation. Most people do not bother to examine small print legal notices on the back pages. In *Mullane* the legal notices did not even state the beneficiaries' names.

Mullane finally obtained a victory—albeit a *partial* victory.

The Supreme Court rejected Mullane's notion that personal service for unnamed parties affected by pending litigation was required. Procedural due process was satisfied if the "form chosen is not substantially less likely to bring home notice than other of the feasible and customary substitutes." But no method of notice was mandated. Instead, the court adopted a two-stage standard for gauging the "best notice practicable." The first step required individualized notice when realistic, such as mailing notice directly to beneficiaries with valid known addresses, or if they could be discovered via reasonable means. If this was not possible, then "constructive notice" sufficed.

The High Court held that the Fifth and Fourteenth Amendments, requiring notice and an opportunity to be heard to parties in a lawsuit, must be "reasonably calculated, under all the circumstances, to apprise interested parties of the pendency of the action and afford them an opportunity to present their objections."

Mullane remains the due process notice gold standard to this day. It continues to guide courts, class action attorneys, and class action administrators, and it provides the procedural underpinnings followed by the drafters of the 1966 FRCP 23 revisions regarding class action notice. *Hansberry* is still constantly cited regarding adequate representation in class actions to determine whether *res judicata* applies.

In 1948 the Supreme Court's *Shelley v. Kraemer* ruling found that restrictive covenants constituted state action and violated the Fourteenth Amendment's equal protection clause. But the holding was limited to preventing courts from enforcing the covenants, not their existence. Homeowners' associations persisted to dissuade their members from selling to Black families.

Lorraine Hansberry, daughter of Carl, wrote the award-winning play *A Raisin in the Sun*, incorporating many of her personal experiences about the home purchase and move into the storyline. The Broadway play received rave reviews and garnered four Tony Award nominations. In 1961 a film version starring Sidney Poitier was released, again receiving deserved critical acclaim.

Today the main street in South Chicago is called Martin Luther King Jr. Drive, renamed three months after his assassination in 1968. The area now is a completely African American neighborhood.

Sadly, Carl Hansberry didn't have a chance to savor his daughter's literary success or the victory of his long-fought cause to eliminate racially restrictive covenants. Frustrated by pervasive racism, he made plans to move his family to Mexico. While making arrangements south of the border, he died of a cerebral hemorrhage, never knowing that the U.S. Supreme Court eventually found the repugnant covenants unconstitutional. Mr. Hansberry, raised in the Mississippi cotton fields, with heroism and persistence leading to a Supreme Court victory, was a great motivator in providing the necessary inspiration and vitality to the budding Civil Rights Movement.

In the next chapter we'll take a good look at the monumental efforts of another civil rights hero, school-aged Linda Brown, who served as the lead plaintiff in one of the greatest class actions of all time, the historic *Brown v. Board of Education*.

Chapter 14

1954: *Brown v. Board of Education*

Traditionally, equity has been characterized by a practical flexibility in shaping its remedies and by a facility for adjusting and reconciling public and private needs. These cases call for the exercise of these traditional attributes of equity power.

—*Chief Justice Earl Warren,*
Brown v. Board of Education, 1954

"This is the first indication I have ever had that there is a God," Supreme Court Justice Felix Frankfurter told a former law clerk regarding the 1953 death of Chief Justice Fred Vinson. Vinson, with a segregationist past, doubted the High Court's authority to order an end to racial segregation. In the early 1950s numerous lawsuits were pending challenging the court's 1896 *Plessy v. Ferguson* "separate but equal" ruling. Frankfurter viewed Vinson's passing as paving the way for favorable decisions in the upcoming education desegregation cases.

President Eisenhower nominated Earl Warren, the conservative Republican governor of California, to replace Vinson. *Brown v. Board of Education* was one of the first cases heard by the Warren Court. The stage was set. In the most important and consequential set of cases in the annals of class action history, the new chief justice stunned the world with his authorship of the court's unanimous decision.

> We conclude that in the field of public education the doctrine of "separate but equal" has no place. Separate educational facilities are inherently unequal. Therefore, we hold that the plaintiffs and others similarly situated for whom the actions have been brought are, by reason of the segregation complained of, deprived of the equal protection of the laws guaranteed by the Fourteenth Amendment.[50]

Equity is utilized when the law cannot provide an adequate solution. Class actions and injunctions, two critical components in the equity toolbox, were employed in force to address America's greatest long-term social problem of race relations. Courts attempted to fill the gap that executive and/or legislative branches were unwilling to address.

Usually, group members 'join' the group: the parishioners in Nuthampstead, the miners in Derbyshire, the privateers, members of the Tribe of Ben-Hur. Others, such as the Methodist Book of Concern beneficiaries, were in the group based on the actions of others. However, African Americans are 'grouped' because of the color of their skin, combined with persistent oppressive treatment after emancipation. Perhaps Black Americans are most similar to the Channel Islanders, with no chance to choose group membership simply because of who they are or where they live.

However, from all these stories, until this point in history, we have yet to feel the full impact, magnitude, and power of class action's beauty to address society's wrongs. Enter Thurgood Marshall, commanding the grand legal strategy leading to the end of America's official policy of segregation. Chief Justice Warren said of Marshall, "If oral argument proved anything, the arguments of Negro counsel proved that they are not inferior. I don't see how we can continue in this day and age to set one group apart from the rest and say that they are not entitled to exactly the same treatment as all others."[51]

Young Thurgood Marshall was initially exposed to the law, oddly enough, because he was a mischievous lad in high school. Upon being sent out of the classroom, he was required to read the Constitution as punishment. Apparently, these punishments were repetitive and, fortunately for us all, an excellent educational device. The ongoing unruly behavior of the future Supreme Court justice provided more than ample opportunities to memorize the document. At the age of thirty-two, he had already won his first Supreme Court case, freeing four young Black males forced to confess because of "police pressure."

Numerous cases followed. As the NAACP's top attorney from 1938 to 1961, Marshall argued and won twenty-nine of the thirty-two civil rights cases before the Supreme Court. Chief Justice Warren would consider Marshall quite "superior."

In the late 1930s, soon after FRCP 23 went into effect, Marshall began his Fourteenth Amendment Equal Protection Clause crusade. Directing the NAACP's legal efforts, he generated the first published class action decision under Rule 23 in a Civil Rights case: a 1941 suit obtaining equal pay for a group of Black schoolteachers and principals in Florida. A succession of similar judicial victories for Black educators throughout the highly segregated Southern states followed. Marshall was already a legend to civil rights activists long before the string of Supreme Court victories.

School desegregation posed a greater challenge. Individual cases would always face the issue of mootness. Each time a student graduated, legal action no longer benefited them. Aiding Black students one at a time could not substantively assist the cause of desegregation. Class actions were necessary. Adding to the difficulty, these cases were brought under the Fourteenth Amendment Equal Protection Clause. These rights were deemed *several* rights, meaning they were personal to the litigant. With the significant social issues involved, courts began taking a more pragmatic approach in desegregation litigation. Equity at play again!

In *Kansas City v. Williams*, a 1953 Eighth Circuit Court of Appeals decision involving Marshall challenging the segregation of Kansas City parks, the tribunal accepted that:

> Violations of the Fourteenth Amendment are of course violations of individual or personal rights . . . where they are committed on a class basis or as a group policy, such as a discrimination generally because of race, they are . . . entitled to be made the subject of class actions.[52]

Courts reasoned that injunctive relief in desegregation cases did not compel absent class members to perform or restrict any action. No controversy within the class was possible. An order approving Blacks to utilize city parks, or permit them to go to all-White colleges, did not require that they engage in any integration activities. Indeed, Black teachers had no reason to protest injunctions ordering higher salaries. These class actions did not interfere with anyone's personal Fourteenth Amendment rights.

For several years the local NAACP and its lawyers sought to persuade the Board of Education of Topeka Public Schools to voluntarily integrate their elementary schools. While Southern states required segregation as a matter of state law, Kansas law did not. When persuasion was unsuccessful, litigation commenced. In civil rights education segregation class action cases recruiting plaintiffs was often necessary and could be difficult. The NAACP sought plaintiff parents whose children attended segregated schools. Those children, as well as the parents, could face myriad forms of harassment within the community because of their involvement in the case. Yet, in 1951, thirteen brave parents agreed to be plaintiffs on behalf of their twenty even braver children.

Oliver Brown, the lead plaintiff for his daughter Linda, was recruited by one of the local NAACP attorneys, a long-time friend. Brown worked as a welder for the Atchison Topeka and Santa Fe Railroad and was an assistant pastor of his church. Because Brown was the only male recruited, he was chosen as lead plaintiff. Besides, it never hurts a case to have a hard-working plaintiff spending his spare time pastoring a church.

Linda was in the third grade. She walked six blocks to the school bus stop. She then traveled one mile to her segregated Black school. The White school was seven blocks from her home. It was not unusual in communities like Topeka that White and Black children would play together in the neighborhood but attend separate schools. However, Linda's circumstances were nowhere near as bad as they were for Black children in some Southern states where no transportation was provided and the Black school was far away.

Ultimately, Linda Brown was designated as the lead student plaintiff in the Supreme Court when a collection of school desegregation cases was docketed. The Topeka parents and their children's cases were combined with parallel NAACP class actions with similarly situated parents and children in Clarendon County, South Carolina, Prince Edward County, Virginia, and New Castle County, Delaware. The case carried little Linda's name first because it was filed first. Linda, and all these children, were all part of a historic class action. Four class actions with many group representatives, combined, standing in for the larger group to create and protect their right to a truly equal education.

Class actions challenging segregation keep the hope and opportunity of equal educational opportunities alive for each Black school child. As we all know, the plaintiffs were victorious. The Supreme Court's landmark class action court decision unanimously ruled that

Linda Brown standing outside Sumner Elementary School, Topeka, Kansas, 1953.

"separate but equal" educational facilities are inherently unequal, depriving these students of the equal protection of the laws guaranteed by the Fourteenth Amendment of the U.S. Constitution.

Left unanswered was how, or when, were courts or school districts to end school segregation? The decision provided no guidance. A year later, in a case dubbed *Brown II*, the court ordered states to desegregate "with all deliberate speed," but, again, offered no particular definition for the meaning of that term. These rulings provided ripe grounds for continued litigation on an issue that would persist for the next two generations.

In response, Southern legislatures quickly passed new restrictive discriminatory practices laws. They were designed to frustrate class action principles by emphasizing class members' differing characteristics, as commonality was the basis of effective desegregation rulings. "Pupil placement laws" were created requiring local school boards to mandate student placement evaluations along with a difficult appeal procedure. Each application was unique and hence could not be addressed on a class action basis. After the board's appeal denied a Black student's assignment request, they were then required first to litigate in segregationist-oriented state courts, and only after exhausting those appeals, to proceed to federal court. Considering the time that this individual process required, the students' cases would be mooted—the entire purpose of the pupil placement laws.

The federal judiciary's patience wore thin as local Southern school boards routinely denied all Black student applications to White schools, making participation in "pupil placement laws" a complete futility. Time most certainly passed for "all deliberate speed." Courts started 're-interpreting' *Brown* to require "systemic integration," not a mere prohibition on discrimination. In response, school districts commenced so-called freedom of choice plans, allowing students to attend any school they liked under the presumption that few Blacks would bother based on harassment, fear, and transportation issues, among other challenges.

Linda Brown (front) and other children of the Brown v. Board of Education *case, Topeka, Kansas, 1950s.*

Resistance also came from Black principals and teachers in all-Black schools. They were concerned that decreasing enrollment would impact their livelihoods. Additionally, Black rural communities financially benefited from governmental programs intended to create more 'equal' separate schools. Hence, the 'class' affected did not necessarily all speak with a single voice, an argument often utilized by civil rights defendants attempting to defeat class action treatment. Civil rights lawyers were also concerned about Black parents desiring their children to attend a segregated school. Whites have bad practices, it was argued. My child should be with their own kind. Reversing racial roles and attitudes is no less troublesome, but, for the sake of the law, Mr. Marshall could not afford divisions within the class.

The reality of enforcing class action court desegregation orders was dramatic. President Eisenhower disagreed with prioritizing school integration, calling it a "terrible mistake." Start first with desegregating parks, cafes, and motels before focusing on sensitive school and educational facility issues. But Ike knew there "must be respect for the Constitution—which means the Supreme Court's interpretation of the Constitution—or we shall have chaos."[53]

In 1957 Arkansas Governor Orval Faubus openly defied a court order to integrate Central High in Little Rock. In response, Eisenhower called in the 101st Airborne and ordered the Arkansas National Guard into federal service to enforce the court's decree.

At the time of the Supreme Court's 1954 *Brown* decision, seventeen states had laws enforcing school segregation. By 1958 only seven states still maintained public school segregation. Southern governors continued to defy federal court integration orders. In 1962 Mississippi Governor Ross Barnett defied federal court orders for James Meredith to attend the University of Mississippi. In response, President Kennedy acted similar to Eisenhower, enforcing court orders by sending in the army and federalizing the Mississippi National Guard.

JFK had to act again, in June 1963, when Alabama Governor George Wallace prevented Blacks from enrolling in the University of Alabama. Months earlier, during Wallace's swearing in ceremony, he pronounced "segregation now, segregation tomorrow, segregation forever." Again, federal troops were sent to enforce the court order. Wallace ultimately backed down.

As we'll see in chapter 16, "1966: The Year Everything Changed," the new FRCP 23 rule altered the landscape for class action injunctions. However, judicial attitudes were already conforming to the new rule before it was finalized and official. A Fifth Circuit opinion written by Judge John Minor Wisdom (yes, his name really was Judge Wisdom), stated that segregation harm "transcend[ed] in importance the harm to individual Negro children," referring to the Fourteenth Amendment rights being considered "several" or personal; that a "separate school system was an integral element in the southern state's general program to restrict Negroes as a class" and keep them in their proper "place." He advised that "adequate redress" of the long history of racial segregation was a "group phenomenon," and "calls for much more than allowing a few Negro children to attend formerly white schools." Wisdom wisely pontificated that wholesale social transformation for the entire class of Blacks was necessary. Hence, these school districts had an affirmative duty to integrate, meaning individual relief alone "will not satisfy the class."[54]

The die for FRCP Rule 23 changes had been cast.

In 1961 Thurgood Marshall was appointed to the U.S. Second Circuit Court of Appeals by President Kennedy, serving until 1965. Thereafter, he was appointed by President Johnson, his drinking buddy, as U.S. solicitor general, representing the U.S. government before the Supreme Court. It was said that "the two men loved to drink bourbon and tell stories full of lies."[55]

In 1966 Marshall lost the government's argument in the famous *Miranda v. Arizona* criminal warnings case (you have the right to remain silent . . .).

LBJ found a way to put Marshall, as the first African American, on the High Court. Associate Justice Tom Clark's son, Ramsey, was appointed U.S. attorney general. Hence, a conflict of interest was created that provoked the father to retire. Johnson was a master at working political and governmental systems.

Marshall's nomination process was not so smooth. He faced Southern senators none too happy with the march of desegregation— and Marshall's role in it. James Eastland of Mississippi, chairman of the Senate Judiciary Committee, was an infamous racist. His father had notoriously lynched a Black couple. Eastland employed more than a hundred Black sharecroppers on his plantation. His daughter had been crowned Miss Confederacy in 1956.

President Johnson worked the phones and ensured that Marshall would be confirmed. In the end, in August 1967, the Senate voted 69 to 11 to place the first Black person on the Supreme Court, with LBJ obtaining many abstentions, instead of *no* votes, from Southern senators.

Marshall served on the High Court for twenty-four years, but it was said that he was much happier as an advocate in the courtroom than sitting as a judge.

In the late 1970s George Wallace publicly apologized to Blacks for his segregationist past. As a born-again Christian, he needed to seek love and forgiveness. "I was wrong. Those days are over, and they ought to be over."[56]

In 1954 no Black students attended school with White students in Southern states. In 1980 40 percent of students in Southern integrated schools were White. Today White students make up 29 percent of integrated Southern classrooms. While Black fourth graders' math scores have improved and are comparable to White averages of the prior generation, the Black-White educational achievement gap remains.

Court-ordered educational desegregation remains elusive to this day as the lack of concurrent residential integration must also be simultaneously addressed. Segregated communities lead to segregated schools. Combining issues of housing and education are simply too overwhelming, even for courts with class action equity powers that enable them to address these matters.

Brown v. Board of Education's greatest legacy is probably in encouraging the Civil Rights Movement, from Rosa Parks and the desegregation of bus lines to lunch counter sit-ins, voter registration drives, and ultimately the Civil Rights Act of 1964 and the Voting Rights Act of 1965.

Linda Brown didn't realize until high school that she would be in history books. Her class was learning about segregation and Supreme Court decisions. Suddenly, her case was being discussed. She had not thought much about her role in this historic case, attending integrated middle and high schools, and she had always played with her many White friends. In her circumstances, winning the case didn't dramatically change her life.

Appropriately enough, she became a Head Start teacher and educational consultant. In 1979 she reopened the Topeka case on behalf of her children with the assistance of the American Civil Liberties Union. She argued that the district's schools were still racially divided. It took until 1993, with a Court of Appeals ruling requiring the district to build three new schools as part of the integration efforts, to obtain victory in that lawsuit.

Linda has told the story that on the first day of school in September 1954, photographers swarmed her classroom. Her classmates were amused that she was the center of attention. When eleven-year-old Linda had advised her classmates of her central role in the famous integration case, "they didn't believe me."[57]

Chapter 15

1961: The One-Way Intervention Controversy

To gild refined gold, to paint the lily . . . is wasteful and ridiculous excess.

—King John, *Act IV, Scene 2*
William Shakespeare, 1595

In 1873 Mark Twain published his first novel, *The Gilded Age: A Tale of Today*, a satire of political corruption and greed in America. The book's title quickly caught the popular imagination, coining the name of the period of 1870 to 1900. This was a time when business tycoons monopolized key industries, such as oil, railroads, finance, and steel, amassing incredible wealth and eliminating competition, while paying workers extremely low wages. The name came from a line in Shakespeare's *King John*—the same King John who granted the Channel Islanders their unique self-governing charter.

Monopolies were not new. The British granted many monopolies in the form of exclusive contracts to colonial administrators as an economic incentive to bring trade to and from the New World. After the

Civil War, rapid industrialization and expansive transformation of the American economy occurred. More than a century later, the leading tycoons are still well-known names: John D. Rockefeller founded Standard Oil; Andrew Carnegie largely built the steel industry; J.P. Morgan reorganized modern banking and helped found General Electric; Cornelius Vanderbilt created railroads and shipping empires.

These great entrepreneurs earned the moniker "robber barons," a term dating from the Middle Ages when questionable ethical practices were employed to eliminate competition and create monopolies for their industry or trade. These mammoth robber baron enterprises squashed small entities struggling to maintain profit margins. In response, Congress passed the Sherman Act of 1890. Its goal: to preserve a competitive marketplace and prevent anticompetitive agreements and unilateral conduct that monopolized or attempted to monopolize the relevant market. The act authorized the Justice Department to bring lawsuits for injunctive relief to halt these practices. Most importantly for the history of class action purposes, private parties were empowered to bring lawsuits for treble damages against anti-competitive monopolies.

In the late 1950s antitrust class actions seeking monetary damages would fall under the *spurious* suit of former FRCP Rule 23(a)(3), discussed in chapter 12, "1936: The Birth of Grandfather 23." Recall that under spurious class actions, no procedural mandate existed directing trial court judges of when or how they were to notify class members of the pending action. In early class action certification procedure, the determination of whether a valid class action existed usually occurred at trial. It was up to the trial judge to determine when class members were to opt in to a spurious lawsuit. But if there was no pre-trial class determination, why would class members even be notified?

This story occurs in the late 1950s. In this antitrust class action, treble damages were sought by thirty-six independent miners against two mining companies. This *spurious* class action was brought under the then-existing FRCP 23(a)(3) for themselves and on behalf of about 350 other similarly situated unnamed miners. At its core, the lawsuit alleged a standard price-fixing conspiracy by defendant corporations to set and depress prices of vanadium and uranium ores purchased from the miners. Seemingly a kinship with the cause of the Derbyshire lead miners in 1676. Importantly, this case well-accented the judicial divide on the issue of an essentially passive invitation to opt in to a class action.

We've all heard about uranium and its usage for medicine, nuclear power, and bombs, but I never heard much about vanadium before researching this book. Of course, it is a mineral. It is named for the Norse goddess of beauty, Vanadis, because of its beautiful colors. The chief domestic source of vanadium is uriniferous sandstone in the Colorado Plateau, the location of our lawsuit. The plateau is an extremely wide area encompassing the Four Corners region of Colorado, Utah, New Mexico, and Arizona. Vanadium has many uses, reducing the weight of and strengthening steel, adding resistance against corrosion and strength to glass, for pigmentation, as a superconductor for magnets, and use in computers, to name a few. Today researchers believe it can even aid diabetics.

I have learned that rarely does a single case act as a fulcrum to examine a perceived flaw in procedural law. Before the 1966 FRCP 23 rule changes, few spurious class actions were filed and found their way to final judgment. Of course, there were judicial concerns that *one-way intervention*, the practice of only notifying class members after a judgment had been entered, was unfair to defendants. No class member would rationally opt in to a judgment on the losing side. And nothing prevented, besides the statute of limitations, a new set of plaintiffs from bringing a new class action on similar or perhaps slightly modified facts and principles as a recently defeated cause. Hence, the argument ran, class members could sit back, just wait for a successful class action judgment, and then opt in.

The unique facts of *Nisley, et al v. Union Carbide & Carbon*, a 1961 case originally heard in the Utah Federal District Court, set off a firestorm in legal circles, ultimately leading to the 1966 FRCP 23 rule change still in existence today regarding class action certification and the opt-out process. These two critical changes, discussed in the next chapter, forever altered the essential underpinnings of class action law, creating the seeds of a class action administration industry I'll discuss in part 3 of this book, which focuses on the future.

The Utah jury's verdict found for the plaintiffs on the issue of liability, awarding money damages to the named plaintiffs, with a special verdict determining the free-market price for vanadium and uranium. A *special verdict* is when a jury makes a specific factual finding. With no early class action certification rules or procedural requirements directing a trial judge when to provide notice to the unnamed putative plaintiffs of the pending litigation, the court waited until the jury's verdict to decide those issues. Hence, at the end of the trial, the federal court ordered that notice be provided to putative class members, easily identifiable from defendants' business records. Each putative member was then granted six months to file a claim before a specially appointed master.

The defendants dutifully filed an appeal in the Tenth Circuit. That court of appeals well-framed the question that would ultimately face the drafters of the 1966 FRCP 23 revisions:

> It is appellants' contention that the procedure adopted by the trial court erroneously authorizes intervention by the unnamed plaintiffs after rendition of a favorable verdict. And we are thus squarely brought to an unresolved question of procedural law, i.e., whether in a class action under Rule 23(a) (3), F.R.Civ.P., non-participating plaintiffs may intervene after determination of defendants' liability, to share in the fruits of a judgment obtained by their participating representatives.

The majority and dissenting opinions well clarified the resulting split in judicial sentiments that the 1966 FRCP 23 Rule Committee was faced with resolving. The Tenth District majority, after analyzing other similar opinions, felt that having "an identifiable class . . . to prove both membership in the class and damages" was satisfactory for the purposes of application of the judgment and applying a claim.

> Undoubtedly this latter solution results in the more expeditious and efficient disposition of litigation and ought therefore to be favored. If, on the other hand, this type of class action was intended to have as its only function an adjunctive method of permissive joinder, there would be no logical reason for its being made a part of [FRCP 23] instead of another means of joinder.

Joinder means bringing lawsuits together.

This court of appeal saw FRCP 23 as having a broad authority and purpose "to allow a final determination of common questions of law and fact." It found great utility to "elucidate the modern-day concepts of class actions." Requiring all parties to be brought before the court before judgment would be "inconsistent with the broad purposes of the Rules."

As these modern-day concepts were, at that time, in transformation, it must be emphasized that this majority opinion considered *one-way intervention* to be *modern day*. Citing to the U.S. Supreme Court opinion in *Hansberry v. Lee*, the appeal court majority pronounced, "One is not precluded from claiming the benefits of a favorable judgment to which he was not a named party, simply because he would not have been bound by an unfavorable judgment rendered against named parties who did not adequately represent his interests."

The court also noted that no final judgment had yet to be decreed and would not occur until the class members opted in. Hence, *res judicata* would not be implicated. Sounds like the judges were also doing some legal maneuvering.

The dissent argued that no cases upheld the rights of *non-appearing* class members being affected by a judgment. That opinion, after reviewing FRCP 23(a)(3)'s history, felt it was nothing more than a permissive joinder device. Citing to the esteemed Professor James Moore, a leading force in the 1936 rule's formulation, the dissent stated:

> The spurious class suit is a permissive joinder device. . . . The character of the right sought to be enforced for or against the class is . . . several, and there is a common question of law or fact affecting the several rights and a common relief is sought. There is no jural relationship between the members of the class; unlike, for example, the members of an unincorporated association, they have taken no steps to create a legal relationship among themselves. They are not fellow travellers by agreement.

Sounds like this judge was reading Sir Edward Coke.

The dissent admitted there "still seems considerable confusion as to the meaning and effect of the third [spurious] group of class actions authorized by" FRCP 23. The question remaining at that time was at what point in the litigation are spurious class members to be included or excluded, a determination left unanswered until the 1966 rule revision.

Despite a clear dispute between various circuits, and even within circuits, regarding the application of one-way intervention in spurious class actions, the Supreme Court refused further review of the case. The High Court never decided the issue either way prior to the promulgation of the 1966 FRCP rule changes.

A 1963 *Harvard Law Review* article analyzing the result in this case recommended that

> Perhaps a better solution would be for the court, at an early stage of the proceedings, to determine whether the pending action was an appropriate one for a judgment encompassing all members, and if so, order notice to the class. Members would have an opportunity to participate, within the bounds of manageability, or to show cause why they should not be included in the judgment.[58]

The committee proposing the 1966 FRCP rule changes also found one-way intervention quite disturbing. Professor Charles Wright, a drafter of the 1966 rule changes, once stated in frustration that a spurious class action is "not really a class action at all."

However, the Utah trial court-approved procedure, upheld by the court of appeals, was never instituted. The parties agreed to a lump-sum settlement before final judgment was entered.

The next chapter is the story of the 1966 rule changes. We are still on that same historical path today, as these rules still govern federal class actions. The committee ultimately selected the *Harvard Law Review* approach cited above, creating the class action certification and notice standard for the last fifty-plus years, and spawning a class action administration industry supporting the drafters' procedural scheme. The embryo has been created.

Chapter 16

1966: The Year Everything Changed

We have come a long, long way but we still have a long, long way to go.
—Dr. Martin Luther King, Jr., speech at Southern
Methodist University, March 17, 1966

Class actions are an American story. We have seen the nation's largest church divide along lines mirroring the regional slavery schism that took place fifteen years before the Civil War, and a Union general's best-selling book morph into an association's quest for protection from Gilded Age greed. We saw the effects of class actions from the Nevada gold mines to the Arkansas coal fields to the Four Corners vanadium fields, leading to sweeping, private antitrust law enforcement action that pitted both workers and smaller capitalists against large mining interests.

We viewed the long struggle and conflict to upgrade the social position of Blacks—from housing in South Chicago to public education throughout the South, and now, in this story, to the meeting rooms of the Supreme Court's Advisory Committee. We witnessed the administration of a trust by a New York bank, the sad end of a Revolutionary War patriot's life, and a most scholarly judge who traipsed the countryside to rule as a one-man, in-the-field court of appeal. These events, affecting both law and culture across the American landscape, lead us to the 1966 revisions of FRCP Rule 23 and the present-day framework of federal class actions in America.

Today, some see class actions as a few rescuing a larger group of those vulnerable and injured by corporate giants, a mass legal remedy for consumers and environmentalists against the blunders or the greed of mass production. Often a small amount of harm is caused to many, which in the aggregate results in large damage to society. An alternative view: greedy lawyers making millions of dollars on the backs of the very groups they purport to represent, while their unknown clients receive a mere coupon in the mail.

Are those attorneys really righteous gladiators fighting for consumers and investors, fighting for civil and workers' rights? What price do we pay for the failings of our capitalist market system? How do we remedy the legislative and executive branches of government's inability or unwillingness to enforce public policy, spurring judicial activism to collectivize law enforcement via class action advocacy?

Depending on your perspective, this is a story of democracy either assigning or abdicating regulatory powers to class action lawyers and unelected judges. These are the people who determine if you are part of a defined class and approve settlements without your consent, often based on a simplified legalism of 'We tried the best we could to find you. Sorry that the postcard never arrived.'

In this story, top-shelf legal scholars and thinkers create a regulatory system of self-selected private attorneys empowered to bring class actions. Unelected judges ultimately grant their class certification motions and approve settlements binding on absent class members.

Pressed into the lawsuit without their acquiescence, commoners lose their right to sue because an unknown lawyer, usually far away, settles their claim. Federal judges, appointed for life, supervise private counsel exercising significant regulatory powers with no accountability to any electorate.

Since we now live in that future, perhaps it's not so scary. Maybe it's a grand, well-conceived plan working as fast as justice permits—the prodigy of the king's equity.

The 1966 FRCP rule changes essentially remain intact to this day. This story mostly takes place in a Supreme Court conference room with decisions made by unelected but highly esteemed law professors, judges, and practitioners. In the mid-1960s those great legal minds conceived a new set of class action procedures to protect all parties and ensure due process, judicial finality, and a coherent, workable class certification procedure. In that Supreme Court meeting room, the rule-makers were creating two species of class actions, and somewhat unknowingly, creating a potent force of private attorneys general, with self-appointed regulatory powers, potentially binding all in their path with a fully enforceable *res judicata* effect.

A major dichotomy in due process was being brewed. In money damages cases, class members must receive notice and an opportunity to opt out. However, in that conference room, the creators conceived the notion that injunctive relief plaintiffs were not required to provide notice or opportunity to opt out, even though in both categories of cases class members were bound by the eventual judgment. The plan was for money damage class members to have control over their fate, while injunctive relief class members would not.

Some nuts and bolts: After World War II, the federal courts workload was increasingly burdened. Society, as always, became more complex than before, more statutes were passed regulating private activity, and state tort laws were expanding. In 1960 Chief Justice

Earl Warren saw the need to act. He reconvened the Advisory Committee on Rules for Civil Procedure under the Rules Enabling Act passed down a generation before, as we saw in chapter 12, "1936: The Birth of Grandfather 23."

Warren appointed a completely new cast of advisors, determined to rewrite court rules for better judicial efficiency. The chief told the committee, "We are falling behind, day by day. In most of the metropolitan centers in keeping up with our judicial functions and certainly one of the great factors in this field is having an adequate and efficient set of rules."[59] The quest for the chief's 'efficient' system was key.

The moniker *Advisory Committee* seems like a misnomer—they are ultimately the decision makers, not mere advisors. Under the Rules Enabling Act, the committee submits its proposed rules, via the chief justice, onto Congress. The legislators then have sixty days to veto the rules. If no action is taken, the rules are activated. In the history of the act, Congress has never acted.

Chief Warren assembled the legal all-stars of the time. As chairman, he selected Dean Acheson, Harry Truman's secretary of state, another individual with remarkable achievements. Acheson managed the Marshall Plan to reconstruct Europe after World War II and the Truman Doctrine to contain the Soviet Union. He was instrumental in creating the North Atlantic Treaty Organization. He is credited with convincing President Truman to intervene in the Korean War. He was certainly a critical player in rearranging the post-war world.

A survey of numerous Acheson online biographies doesn't indicate his participation as chairman of the advisory committee. His position in my little history storybook appears to be discounted when compared to saving the Western world on numerous fronts. Understandable.

Warren's appointments were top-heavy with anti-segregationist litigators. However, there is no indication that this was his goal. He most likely just chose the most highly qualified, intelligent lawyers who had previously used their superior skills in addressing the moral imperative of the day.

Benjamin Kaplan was appointed as lead reporter, responsible for drafting the rules in accordance with the committee's directives. After World War II Kaplan had served as a Nuremberg prosecutor of Nazi war crimes, including the Holocaust. His boss was Supreme Court Associate Justice Robert Jackson, appointed as lead U.S. Nuremberg prosecutor for the United States. The United Kingdom, the Soviet Union, and France each had a chief prosecutor as well. Kaplan was charged with drafting indictments bridging three separate legal traditions: the Anglo-American, the French, and the Russian. This was a perfect training ground for him, as he was later tasked with drafting federal rules after discussions with numerous experts.

Kaplan taught civil procedure at Harvard Law and was a veteran of human rights causes. He assisted the NAACP with *Shelley v. Kraemer* and was Thurgood Marshall's chief source of law clerks during his time on the Second Circuit Appeals Court.

Albert Sacks clerked for Justice Felix Frankfurter before spending forty years at Harvard Law School—twenty years on the faculty and another twenty as dean. He also worked with the NAACP, marching with Martin Luther King, Jr., in August 1963, just before the "I Have a Dream" speech, while the Advisory Committee was actively performing its redrafting tasks. It's fair to say he was motivated.

Charles Alan Wright was the lone Southerner among the key 1966 authors. He opposed Texas's newly created pupil placement laws, which I discussed in chapter 14, "1954: *Brown v. Board of Education*." He steered the campaign to desegregate the Texas Episcopal Church, as well as his children's private school.

However, Wright was more than a local activist and lawyer. I might put him on the all-time, all-star legal team. He was co-author of the fifty-four-volume treatise *Federal Practice and Procedure* (Wright and Miller). All I can say is, "Move over, Joseph Story!"

Not convinced? When President Richard Nixon was faced with congressional investigations regarding the Watergate break-in and coverup, he retained Wright as special legal consultant. For a time, he was also the president's lead lawyer.

Rough-and-tumble Arizonan John Frank was a different breed from the other leading authors. He was a private litigator from the desert west, bringing a unique perspective to the deliberations. Frank was a stern believer in protecting individual rights. He viewed class actions as potentially removing those individual rights.

At the tender age of twenty-five, Frank was Justice Hugo Black's only law clerk. During World War II, Japanese Americans were placed under military curfew. The constitutionality of these detentions was challenged. Frank strenuously appealed to Black to nullify the curfew, arguing, "In America guilt must be personal and that no man should be convicted because of his associations."

The court unanimously found the curfew constitutional.

Frank later became involved in the Civil Rights Movement, advising Thurgood Marshall and the NAACP to challenge the constitutionality of racial segregation. Frank was co-counsel for Ernesto Miranda in the famed *Miranda* criminal warning case, squaring off against his friend Marshall, who at the time was serving as solicitor general.

The committee was comprised of other legal luminaries as well: George Doub, the former assistant attorney general of the Civil Division at the Department of Justice; Charles Edward Wyszynski, Jr., former solicitor of labor for the Justice Department, and special assistant in the office of the solicitor general. Wyszynski was nominated to the federal bench by FDR a week before Pearl Harbor and confirmed by the Senate two weeks later. Pretty darn efficient. The lineup also included Grant Cooper, former president of the American College of

Trial Lawyers. He later defended Sirhan Sirhan, Senator Robert F. Kennedy's assassin.

Before the new rules were adopted, class actions were still a novelty, as compared to today, a constant of the litigation landscape. Indeed, the drafters of the 1966 FRCP 23 rule changes internal memoranda noted that, in the prior decade, only about a dozen class action federal appellate opinions were filed each year. The same limited volume held true in state courts. Today it is possible that a dozen federal class action opinions of one form or another could be issued in a single week.

America was a different place in the first half of the 1960s than it was in the second. The core of the 1966 rule changes that are substantively similar today were finalized in February 1964. The Advisory Committee had no way of knowing the far-reaching legal, political, cultural, and social changes brewing just around the corner.

The Johnson administration had not yet obtained passage of civil rights, employment, and voting rights laws. The Vietnam War was a minor sideshow. Nonexistent was the wide array of consumer protection and environmental legislation later passed in the Nixon administration. These cases formed the foundation for the first swell of class actions leading to large law firms prosecuting and defending mega-sized class actions years into the future. Oh yes, on February 9, 1964, the Beatles appeared on the *Ed Sullivan Show* for the first time.

The heart of the class action litigation 'industry' at the time was integration lawsuits. As discussed above, many committee members were personally involved in desegregation battles, an area of deep concern and experience to the drafters. These key players' deep motivation, with pen and typewriter at hand, used their positions and opportunities to create a litigation framework with which to attack racial segregation. One internal memo stated, "[I]t is absolutely essential to the progress of integration that such suits be treated as class actions, with the judgment binding on all members of the class . . . we must take care of these cases [and] must . . . make it absolutely clear that the desegregation cases . . . are covered."[60]

Of course, they could not forget their primary goal, as instructed by Chief Warren: Craft a clean, flexible rule reflecting some courts' newer approaches to numerous civil procedure rules, not just class actions. The court transmitted five rule changes in 1961 and twenty-four more in early 1963. Although the committee was formed in 1960, the more difficult task of class action rules was finally discussed and debated in 1963.

One of the first issues resolved required a court to make a class action certification decision "at an early practicable time after a person sues or is sued as a class representative." No rule then existed regarding when a court should make such a determination. The committee sought to force trial court judges to manage class actions in the formative stages of the litigation. An early certification decision was a fair and efficient procedure depriving absent class members of the opportunity to wait for a favorable judgment before intervening. The committee and the new rules would jettison the *one-way intervention* rule for good.

If a trial judge was forced into a relatively 'early' certification determination, then Chief Warren wanted clean, flexible rules to guide those courts. So the committee next dealt with commonality, typicality, and the question of whether plaintiff counsel's experience was adequate to prosecute the case. The 1937 rule already accounted for the numerosity and adequacy of the class representative requirement. Commonality involves whether the law and facts are alike for all class members. Here, the focus is on the class definition, not the class representative. A standard commonality circumstance is where all members purchase the same allegedly defective product. Typicality focuses on the class representatives' claim: Does it arise from the same event, practice, or course of the defendant's conduct that also gives rise to class members' claims, and is it based on the same legal theory? This requirement ensures that the class representative will vigorously prosecute the case for the benefit of the entire class.

Regarding representation, the federal trial courts had a new requirement: Does plaintiff's counsel have adequate experience and training to handle the admittedly complex task of prosecuting a class action? An attorney handling traffic cases for a few years is a different breed from a battle-scarred anti-trust or securities litigator.

No requirement regarding class action defense counsel's abilities was discussed or exists, even today.

We humans often set aside difficult issues. No different with our all-star legal team. With the tough questions of class-wide notice, and the opt-out procedure looming, the committee next tackled the infrequently arising issue of protecting defendants from inconsistent rulings.

Class actions are usually thought of as benefiting wide groups of plaintiffs. But in certain circumstances, defendants seek to convert lawsuits against them into class actions for their own benefit. Consider when a defendant is served with numerous similar independent lawsuits by stock or bond holders, or adjacent or same area landowners, or insurance policy holders, all challenging a defendant's actions, or lack of action. The lawsuits are pretty much all the same. But different individual actions could produce risks to defendants of conflicting rulings, not to mention repetitive, burdensome legal costs. Businesses want finality on legal issues destined to be repeated.

The new Rule 23 was designed, as a practical matter, to allow a court to consolidate these claims, along with similar rights or duties, and have them designated as a class action with *res judicata* effect to non-participating parties. Any plaintiff could have brought the matter as a class action, but no one elected to do so. If any plaintiff or the Channel Island judge can decide whether a case should be a class action, why can't a defendant have the same decision-making authority? Under the new rules, the defendant now has that same option. They do not have to keep litigating the same issue again and again, facing the possibility of inconsistent rulings. This approach is consistent with the now-established concept that a judgment can extinguish a person's right to sue without their actual participation in the litigation, so long as someone else adequately represents their interests.

Probably the largest question the Advisory Committee faced involved due process rights for injunctive relief classes. The prevailing side of the argument goes like this: Due process does not require notice and opt-out rights in injunctive relief suits because these remedies promise no practical benefit to absent class members. Refraining comes at no practical cost. When a court enjoins a defendant who acts "on grounds that apply generally to the class," as the new rule requires, no individualized remedy exists. A court could not enjoin enforcement of a juvenile curfew ordinance on First Amendment grounds, for example, then craft an injunction that benefits only certain teenagers. Remedial indivisibility means that individuals who sit on the sidelines, in practical effect, have their rights adjudicated, whether they are class members or not. The right to exclude themselves from litigation gives absent class members no benefit. They also suffer no harm from being forced into the class.

Closer to home, consider the Black family in an education integration class action that does not desire their children to change schools. Or consider an extreme case: a prisoner, while incarcerated, opposing a class action against cruel and unusual punishment because he's a masochist. Shouldn't this person's individual rights be protected? Remember, the committee is packed with anti-segregationists. The revision committee was mindful that some Black putative class members would object to desegregation, being more comfortable sending their children to segregated schools. These objections, if revealed, would play into racist defenders' arguments that class actions were inappropriate for these cases, possibly even a death knell to integration efforts.

The counter argument: A school desegregation suit does not address a single student's personal right to attend a specific school. Rather, there is no alternative but to resolve the problem for all similarly situated children. The uniformity of all the students' claims requires that the decision essentially resolves them all on the merits. The indivisible nature of an integration injunction inevitably influences all children equally.

This had to be simpler when the king made the decisions.

This indivisibility concept has ownership ramifications. Under such circumstances, Benjamin Kaplan argued, "A claim cannot be thought to belong to an individual plaintiff." However, while "giving notice . . . may enable the court to render a judgment with full binding effect when otherwise it could not effectively do so," but "the grand criterion" for a binding "class action" in an injunctive relief case "remains the homogenous character of the class."[61]

The committee determined and validated important Fourteenth Amendment rights and required systemic integration, or the treatment of Black students as groups, regardless of their individual preferences. This result required class treatment of claims. It is human nature; classes would inevitably include dissenting members. So a perfect "harmony of interests" threshold precluded class-wide treatment anytime class member choices became relevant.

Bottom line: The doctrinal foundation for the class-wide *res judicata* for injunctive relief class actions was to facilitate desegregation litigation. However, committee members were mindful that pushback could occur if the rule were couched as a goal to hasten desegregation.

Remember, the Rules Enabling Act mandated that these procedural rules "shall not abridge, enlarge or modify any substantive right." So the committee's "Commentary" seemingly sought to mask their true intent, stating:

> Even if it has taken effect or is threatened only as to one or a few members of the class, provided it is based on grounds which have general application to the class. Subdivision (b)(2) is not limited to civil-rights cases. Thus an action looking to specific or declaratory relief could be brought by a numerous class of purchasers, say retailers of a given description, against a seller alleged to have undertaken to sell to that class at prices higher than those set for other purchasers, say retailers of another description, when the applicable law forbids such a pricing differential (FRCP 23, Notes of Advisory Committee on Rules—1966 Amendment).

Injunctive relief class actions are far more prevalent than money damages class actions. While Professor Wright predicted that the money damages opt-out rule would have little impact, in the end it became the most consequential part. Add on the fact that big money settlements always assure media attention. Wright's error was reasonable considering the state of American law and politics at the time. He could never have foretold the rapidly changing historical perspective that the future would bring.

The money damages rules were completely rewritten to eliminate the defective spurious class action in the original Rule 23. The old rule was not designed to adjudicate the rights or liabilities of nonparties. Hence, the committee created the class issues predominating over individual issues criteria, more technically entitled "Common Question of Law and Fact Predominate and Superior to Adjudicate." That title sounds like seventeenth-century verbiage. From their "Commentary":

> The court is required to find, as a condition of holding that a class action may be maintained under this subdivision, that the questions common to the class predominate over the questions affecting individual members. It is only where this predominance exists that economies can be achieved by means of the class-action device. In this view, a fraud perpetrated on numerous persons by the use of similar misrepresentations may be an appealing situation for a class action, and it may remain so despite the need, if liability is found, for separate determination of the damages suffered by individuals within the class. On the other hand, although having some common core, a fraud case may be unsuited for treatment as a class action if there was material variation in the representations made or in the kinds or degrees of reliance by the persons to whom they were addressed (FRCP 23, Notes of Advisory Committee on Rules—1966 Amendment).

The committee was concerned about collusion between defendant companies and unscrupulous plaintiffs' lawyers who would 'sell' a low settlement for quick substantial fees. Hence, the present-day early certification requirement includes court approval of representation of class counsel *and* of the settlement. To deal with both issues, and the concern about one-way intervention, it was decided that money judgments must be binding on all absent class members with *Mullane* due process protection, providing putative class members notice and an opportunity to opt out.

A storybook including the last fifty years of class action history would certainly tell a different tale than the drafters of FRCP 23 ever expected. The opt-out opportunity expanded class actions to an unforeseen level of participation, creating the need for a separate new industry—class action administration—to act as a notice mailing and clearing house, locating putative class members as well as processing all attendant monetary claims.

Of important note, the committee provided early appeal rights for class action certification decisions. The losing party on a class certification motion was granted an opportunity to petition the appeal circuit for the right to an early appeal. Litigation need not proceed on this crucial decision prior to final judgment and then wait for an appeals court rule on this critical issue.

The world changed quickly after the Advisory Committee finished its work on Rule 23 in 1964. When the TV show *Lost in Space* previewed in 1965, it was shot in black and white. By the 1966 season, it was shot in color. No one foresaw Beatlemania, the vast impact of the Vietnam War and the Civil Rights Movement, or the grand changes in medicine, science, technology, computers, and the internet completely changing the face of class actions today.

The Advisory Committee wrote Rule 23 in a more innocent world. In 1969 famed consumer advocate Ralph Nader hailed, "The exquisite congruence of sanction and relief . . . is implicit in the consumer class action." Many championed Rule 23 as a substitute for an inefficient federal bureaucracy.

Major legislative acts soon followed that fit quite nicely into the newly approved rule: the 1967 Age Discrimination in Employment Act, the 1968 Truth in Lending Act, the 1970 Fair Credit Reporting Act, the National Environmental Policy Act and the Clean Air Act Amendments, the 1972 Clean Water Act, the 1975 Fair Credit Billing Act, and the 1978 Fair Debt Collection Practices Act. These were the foundations long before large-scale consumer and data breach class actions dominated the field.

While the Advisory Committee worked in that Supreme Court conference room, it is said that corporate interests were asleep at the wheel, never realizing the importance that the new rule for money damages class actions would have on the nation's largest business concerns, or that this would lead to the creation of a whole new level of legal entrepreneurship—the birth of the class action administration industry.

The following closing chapters tell the perhaps never-before-told story of the rise of this administrative arm unknowingly created by the 1966 drafters. It provided one of the most powerful leveling legal tools society has created. It came just in time, too, as the technological advances we have come to love and depend on have also endangered our personal freedoms in ways no one could have anticipated in the sixties.

Part III
The Future

*From Mullane to the Great Technological Threat:
Group Representation Protecting
Other Freedoms*

Chapter 17

The World of Group Litigation: Prologue to the Future

For those of us who believe in physics, the distinction between past, present and future is only a stubbornly persistent illusion.
—*Albert Einstein, March 1955*

Before we gaze into the future, we must first appreciate that the 1966 framers had no idea that practically everyone, at some point, and perhaps too often, would be affected by the rules they created. Consider that probably every reader of legal age has received class action notices. The framers unknowingly cut the ribbon launching of a *Mullane*/class action administration notice industry juggernaut of due process providers.

The early consumer cases of the 1970s were faced with the immense challenges of locating class action members, notifying them of potential claims, evaluating the claims, and then disbursing the funds. I have had the privilege over the last twenty years of interacting with many of the early class action administration pioneers and to absorb their deep historical perspectives of the last forty years of this industry. I sought to interview them for this book. Sadly, due to the passage of time, I was unable to either find or receive a response from many of those who have moved on to quieter times later in life. Instead, I embarked on combining my personal knowledge of class action administration and much deeper viewpoints of group representation acquired during the years of working on this book. I also examined similar practices of collateral enterprises since the 1950s, such as direct mail marketing and skip tracing, and how these tools have evolved into being part of the current high-tech due process notice and claims processing industry.

Let's begin with the mail: postal mail, in an envelope, with a stamp, that a governmental officer carries to your home or office. Long before class action notices, the roads carried the message, or the mail. The Romans started their historic road building programs around 500 BC, ultimately connecting continents and spanning more than 250,000 miles from northern England to Egypt. Their transportation/communication system is credited by historians with enabling the spread of the Christian gospel throughout Europe. Roads were the internet of the past.

The 1777 U.S. Articles of Confederation authorized the national government to establish post offices but not post roads to carry the mail. The U.S. Constitution of 1789, Article I, section 8, is the "postal clause," authorizing Congress "to establish post offices and post roads." Our nation's teacher, Justice Joseph Story, pronounced a broad interpretation of the clause in his influential *Commentaries on the Constitution of the United States* (1833) to include all public highways. His liberal interpretation lasts to this day.

From the time of *Mullane* until quite recently the mail was, overwhelmingly, the largest information conduit of litigation information to the potential or actual class action members, with newspapers and magazines trailing far behind. Regarding group representation, to this day, the U.S. Postal Service remains the primary means to notify class action members.

Class action members are located essentially by using the same strategies that direct mail houses utilize in seeking potential customers for their products or services: creating the best possible *prospect list*. Mail-order entrepreneurs understood the power of list building, spawning an industry of *list brokers*—companies that developed mail-order lists for sale. For every transaction conducted by mail—requesting information on vacation properties in Florida, sending in the warranty card for a new RCA television, entering a sweepstakes, buying a set of encyclopedias or a certain type of insurance policy—the consumer's name was placed on one mailing list or another. For list brokers, generating lists had become so lucrative that some companies began aiming simply to break even on the sale of merchandise through the mail, knowing that the real profit lay in renting out their list of names.

A 1989 *Harper's Magazine* article wryly commented:

> We and a thousand other companies are going to appropriate your name, match it, store it, rent it, swap it; we'll evaluate your geo-demographic profile, determine your ethnic heritage, calculate your propensity to consume. We'll track you for the rest of your consuming life—pitch you baby toys when you're pregnant, condos when you're fifty.[62]

These entrepreneurs sought insight into our private lives. Before the computer age, this may have been of little concern to most. But today the likes of Google, Microsoft, and Facebook have entered the grand Faustian bargain—their customers pay nothing for the right to use the service in return for allowing these internet giants to obtain almost unlimited knowledge of our product and life interests. It's the same goal that mass marketers of past generations had. However, back then, obtaining the data was not as easy as it is today.

In the old days, before cheap and simple computer data management, creating and maintaining an accurate list of tens of thousands or a million or more names and addresses, and finding the common threads, would have been prohibitively expensive for many firms. For instance, when *Reader's Digest* planned to mail twenty million subscription solicitations in the 1950s, the firm needed to 'rent' between four hundred and five hundred mailing lists from various sources. Then there was the task of searching for and eliminating the duplicates on those lists, making sure the three to four million existing subscribers were not offended by receiving introductory offers or prospective customers were not receiving duplicate mailings.

This was complicated business that required an enormous amount of tedious and costly labor, requiring scores upon scores of operators with blue pencils sitting at long tables crossing off names from index cards. Once purged by hand, the lists then required an army of home typists producing reams of address labels for the next round of mailings. Machinery was required to address an envelope, duplicate, and sign the letter in blue or black ink, add in the name and address at the top of the letter, fold the letter and insert it into the envelope with enclosures, and finally, seal and mail the envelope.

Back then, information about consumers remained relatively scarce. City directories had long been valuable sources of names and addresses in urban areas but offered little information aside from neighborhood or ward data. Names and addresses could be culled from manufacturers' warranties, state vehicle and voter registration records, and magazine subscriptions. But such lists varied greatly in their quality and accuracy.

As a kid, I recall receiving the Sears catalog and feeling that it was so great that I could just flip the pages, point to the stuff I wanted, and ask my parents to buy it for me. Of course, I never thought for a moment that Sears kept track of me or my family's buying habits. We were just happy to have the catalog and pick things out. Too bad they couldn't innovate, or they might still be a major retailer today.

When I was eighteen years old, I started a silkscreen T-shirt business. I ordered one item from one catalog, and boom, I was on every clothing and merchandising catalog list out there. I was stoked. I was getting great ideas from these catalogs. I never thought to consider why I was receiving them. Now the reason is obvious.

I was one of millions proving that direct mail was a potent instrument for reaching consumers in the crowded marketplace of post-Depression American life. Marketing studies during that time focused upon location, recency of purchase, frequency of purchase, unit of sale, etc., to target mailings. Department store sales slips were constantly reviewed. Did they live in this town or that town? Shop in one or different departments on the same day? How often did they shop? New technologies of storing, sorting, and analyzing information, now considered primitive, transformed the buying and selling of services and products and turned information about consumers into a commodity itself. First, it was the mailbox, then reels and reels of analog magnetic tapes, and later still, spinning disks in hard drives that became the prime avenues for studying consumers and their changing interests. This data collection led to the creation of individualized direct mail marketing. It was the same basic framework that the internet giants now employ, but without the efficiency of modern server farms processing your Google searches or Facebook "likes."

Magnetic tapes loaded with addresses of subscribers, club members, and mail order buyers were the heart of the gestating digital transformation of the direct mail industry. Of course, every entrepreneur wants to know as much as possible about their potential customers. Due to the digital transformation of these antiquated methodologies, we are almost literally offered products and services before we even know we want them. But, hey, maybe that's not so great. More on this subject later.

American consumers had long distinguished themselves from one another based on our consumption behavior, but it would be our habits of reading, donating, and subscribing that those marketers learned to study closely. From my earliest days in the industry, being able to locate class action members by their interests and buying patterns was critical in notifying them so that the *Mullane* standard "to apprise interested parties" of the pending action and their possible claim could be obeyed.

Way back when, veteran professional skip tracers and marketers would buy phone books on giant floppy disks. We followed that model, buying disks that contained driver's license information and others that contained all sorts of licensing and permitting information, such as for fishing or hunting. Back then, skip-tracing companies had to review each of these hundreds of drives before they built the massive off-the-shelf databases. The industry at this time was faced with disparate hardware and software applications, creating a lot of strain on our and other organizations' ability to utilize the data. This grew more prolific in the late 1990s when data companies, such as Accurint, started selling their centralized information services that were easy to use, packaged in a constructive way—the way we wanted.

As part of my investigation into the history of mass mailing, I reached out to Michael McIntosh, a skip-tracing expert. He recounted to me that he would simply start by creating a database with a name and Social Security number on a bulletin that came to be known as a *knowledge index*, which was painfully slow. He advised me that credit-reporting agency TRW (later renamed Experian) then offered a mainframe service with change of address raw data they were acquiring from utilities and magazines. Stanford University set up the ability to search through local voter registration and DMV records, all now governed by different state laws as to the purpose of their usage. This was all before the U.S. Postal Service's national change-of-address system really started or was finalized so that search and update of information could be performed much more quickly.

By modern standards, this system was flawed by the "fire and forget" model. McIntosh advised that once mailed, you lost control. You had no idea who actually received it. You could keep track of it based on who decided to participate, but the mail-order house had no idea as to whether the mailing was an effective way of communicating or contacting that party. Today we can fire and track mail pieces to the final delivery point or, if it was undeliverable, have that knowledge immediately—the very essence of satisfying the *Mullane* standard.

McIntosh also explained that companies gave away products simply for database collection purposes. Provide your contact information to receive free items. Sound like a familiar business model? The history of database marketing is based on the same driving force to obtain all the information that is used today by the internet giants. So much information was gathered that only a few companies could figure out how to aggregate all the data.

In the class action administration context, the two situations where aggregating data can lead to problems are (1) when the initial data received is faulty for some reason (which is usually the ways defendants' systems disgorge the data), without any intent to disrupt claims processing, and (2) when we try to correct duplicate, incomplete, incorrect, or otherwise erroneous data in a data set, called *data cleaning* or *data scrubbing*. A scrubber is trying to fix essentially 'broken' data.

Functionally, some attorney clients would just say, "Mail to everybody at every address on that list, every name we provided to you." Others would say, "Scrub and we'll try to determine the newest address in the data provided." The third option is that before the mailing, we run a *skip trace* with the newest address provided from the U.S. Postal Service National Change of Address (NCOA) data base.

We looked to the history of skip tracing and stumbled upon twentieth-century privacy issues that seemingly now dwarf our twenty-first-century privacy concerns. A *skip* is a person whose whereabouts cannot readily be ascertained, either intentionally or not, or is possibly deceased. Traditionally, skip tracers were, and still are, debt collectors. They could be a bounty hunter for a bail bondsman, or law enforcement tracking down a criminal suspect. Mail order businesses want to locate you to sell a product or service. A skip tracer is looking for you to collect money you owe. A class action administrator is *looking for you to give you money,* usually for a claim you did not even know existed. While the skip tracer is trying to find you in order to get paid, obviously, but more desirably, a class action administrator's goal is exactly the opposite; we usually want to find you in order to give notice of your rights or money. But, essentially, with direct mailers and skip tracers, the processes are all the same.

Since the early days of mail order, marketers have wanted to know your private contact information and purchasing habits. But today anyone can go online, enter a name or telephone number, and be inundated with online services that not only help you find that person but their entire residential and work history, even their relatives and neighbors. Many view these industries as a graver threat than governmental and military power intrusions.

A survey of debt collection manuals from the 1960s found a much different way of life than today, with its own privacy concerns. It seems from reading these antiquated manuals, however, that no one was really all that worried. Of course, people move, and in the debt-collection business the first determination was whether the target was "on the run" or just lackadaisical in notifying others of life changes.

A debt collector searches, to some degree, based upon profitability. In those old days, before privacy statutes and the internet, a debt collector would simply call the last known employer with the ruse of a credit application, to confirm if the "skip" still worked there and to verify the home address. If the employer said they were gone, the skip tracer then would take the role of the employer, calling a possible lead and saying that they were from the personnel department trying to track down the former employee to whom they owed money. They would even visit neighbors and keep track of relatives. Or they would represent themselves as everything from insurance agents to auto financers seeking loan approval. They would call medical offices, utilities, and trade associations using a ruse to find the debtor. Within the industry it was called *tracing with subterfuge*. It was a much more personal game than collectors are forced to use in the modern world of "digital fingerprints." A notable ruse would be to send a telegram with money deliverable only to the addressee. If Western Union said they showed identification, you found the "skip." Paying a "skip" a little money was just one form of "tracing with subterfuge."

There was a time that forwarding addresses from the post office would require writing a check for one dollar per name. Hundreds, maybe thousands of checks for one dollar per name would be sent to obtain forwarding addresses prior to automation. Then the post office created the NCOA and the old mail "fire and forget" model was gone. Necessity being the mother of invention, I spent decades building a company that has, as one of its many features, a unified platform that integrates with the U.S. Postal System where it can fire and track a single mail piece from our mail room to almost the last mile and the final delivery point in the U.S. If the piece is undeliverable, the software platform now instantly performs a skip trace and remail. Now, we cannot forget.

It used to be that cell phone numbers weren't readily available. In order to collect these, we utilized *data aggregators*—leading credit reporting agencies like Equifax, Experian, and TransUnion—that collect data from multiple sources and then repackage the information in a usable form. Sometimes the data provided worked perfectly with our needs. Other times we would have to go through the data name by name or send off *our* aggregated data to other aggregators for processing. Nowadays anyone can find your cell number if they really need it. The moment you sign up or buy anything, your cell phone number is hooked in.

Recall the "frankpledge" discussed in chapter 2, "1199: Rector Sues His Parishioners," that held a group together? In the Middle Ages it was easy to locate the sought-after group members. If the pastor wanted to sue his church members, the word got around and everybody knew. No need for mail, skip tracing, or computers. Of course, no digital threat. But today our groups are usually defined by technology, such as everyone registering the same consumer warranty, owning stock shares in the same company, purchasing from Amazon, etc.

Every technological solution creates a new problem. It seems that almost daily we hear that a data breach—the evil that is always lurking—steals millions of bits of private data, causing credit and privacy issues that many companies are unwilling to spend the resources on to protect. There is no lack of tech entrepreneurs out there, but rest assured that they are not universally nice, caring, wholesome people. Many are unconcerned about the privacy of the people whose data they hold or who consider the possible liabilities and penalties as just the cost of doing business when compared to the possibility of making untold profits. Then there are the purveyors of ransomware, whose goal is essentially to kidnap critical data or entire operating systems from hospitals or utilities that businesses or government too often cannot protect. All of this creates gigantic new vistas of future group representation actions.

We willingly permit Google Maps to track our movements. The collectivized data obtained provides us all with important traffic conditions. Google Maps is also great when used to locate criminals and find out who dumped a body in the trash bin, but we don't necessarily like that Google knows when we went to the Chinese restaurant or when we're out of town. Conversely, when we forget where the Chinese restaurant we went to three weeks ago was, Google Maps is great.

We search online for vitamins, and then get inundated with vitamin ads in our feed. From the historical perspective, group representation used to be the people in the congregation or the miners in England. Now, these class actions could be thirty, forty, fifty or one hundred million people because of the nature of our technological world. But what else is going to protect these millions of people except for class actions? What is going to protect our freedom?

Ransomware poses perhaps one of the biggest problems. We very much appreciate that our medical files are easily accessible to doctors in many locations, or that they can be sent for review to specialists in Boston or Israel. But think now about when ransomware attacks a hospital. Then there is forty-two-year-old Mary, a mother with school-aged kids, lying in a hospital bed and her doctor cannot access her files because there are no longer paper records. Ransomware is signing her death warrant. We must protect Mary so that her kids have a mom to grow up with. These reoccurring attacks become prime fodder for this new emerging area of group representation through class action lawsuits.

The next chapter explores how computing saved our civilization from one of the greatest evils we have known but has also replaced it with an equally grave (possibly greater) threat that can often go beyond our control and even threatens our very existence.

Chapter 18

Freedom Threatened

We go tomorrow.
—Supreme Allied Commander General Dwight (Ike)
D. Eisenhower after being handed intelligence gener-
ated by the first programmable electronic computer,
June 5, 1944[63]

Before World War II a team of British postal engineers had been working on "switching electronics"—using telephones for electronic messages. Once the war commenced, their role changed quickly to decoding the German High Command encrypted messages. The team was aided by a German message operator's mistake—sending two versions of the same message, using the same machine settings—a breakdown in Third Reich security protocol.

In December 1943 the team finalized Colossus, the world's first programmable electronic computer with the capacity to process 1,250 characters of data every second. It was built primarily to decipher the Nazi *Lorenz* code used by senior personnel, as opposed to the more famous *Enigma* codes, used by field units, made famous by the 2014 movie *The Imitation Game.* Colossus I ran on eighteen hundred vacuum tubes. Before this, the most sophisticated device used about 150.

On June 1, 1944, a much-improved version, Colossus II, became functional, running on twenty-four hundred vacuum tubes and processing five thousand characters of data per second. Colossus provided a thorough awareness of German forces in and around Normandy, including troop, vehicle, and tank levels, even maintenance and serviceability information. It was also able to determine that Hitler was personally directing German military strategy. The dawn of data processing had arrived just in time to defeat the Nazis.

On June 5, 1944, General Eisenhower was handed decoded communications intercepted directly from Hitler. The führer believed the buildup of troops in southern England was nothing but a ruse, that the Allies would never attempt crossing the English Channel. Upon receiving this new age computer-decrypted intelligence, Ike decreed, "We go tomorrow." On June 6, 1944, the Normandy invasion commenced.

The fate of the free world hinged on computer-generated intelligence for the first time. Eisenhower later commented that the war would have lasted two years longer if not for the Colossus team's information. This historical sequence is a metaphor for the critical roles of data collection, mind-bending processing speeds that we have come to expect, and security/identification verification present in every group representation case today. During WWII, British Intelligence obtained the data, Colossus delivered the speed of analysis, and the German operators provided the security lapse enabling a successful Normandy invasion. Nowadays, Google and Amazon Web Services obtain the data and provide the speed of analysis, and the local IT departments' security lapses enable the ransomware and data breach bad guys use to perform their evil craft.

Six years later the Supreme Court decision in *Mullane*, which I discussed in chapter 13, "1940–1950: Due Process Trumps Racially

Restrictive Covenants," required that notice must be "reasonably calculated, under all the circumstances, to apprise interested parties of the pendency of the action and afford them an opportunity to present their objections." *Mullane* further ruled that procedural due process is satisfied if the "form chosen is not substantially less likely to bring home notice than other of the feasible and customary substitutes." It was not that far afield from the "customary rights" we saw in chapter 2, "1199: Rector Sues his Parishioners." But the Supreme Court did not mandate any standardized notice method, instead emphasizing flexibility with a two-tier standard to evaluate the best notice practicable. Individualized notice is compulsory when "realistic."

Of course, the 1950 *Mullane* court did not envision or consider the 1966 opt-out rules, or that the presence of computers would ultimately dispense with previously long-held customary standards while creating threatening privacy challenges that are the vanguard of future massive class actions in America. This joining of marketing and communications technology has unknowingly shaped the direction of my class action administration enterprise journey, especially how these advances relate to *Mullane*'s mandate to locate putative class members in money-damages cases, while pursuing "best practicable notice"— meaning massive amounts of mail of all genres.

General Eisenhower could not have envisioned or cautioned us about all the data collection and retention, along with the vast array of privacy and security issues, our computer age would bring. President Eisenhower is not thought of as a "futurist," but he cautioned about the power of our nation's military industrial complex. As he said in his January 17, 1961, farewell presidential address:

> As we peer into society's future, we—you and I, and our government—must avoid the impulse to live only for today, plundering for our own ease and convenience the precious resources of tomorrow. We cannot mortgage the material assets of our

grandchildren without risking the loss also of their political and spiritual heritage. We want democracy to survive for all generations to come, not to become the insolvent phantom of tomorrow.

Today, the solitary inventor, tinkering in his shop, has been overshadowed by task forces of scientists in laboratories and testing fields. In the same fashion, the free university, historically the fountainhead of free ideas and scientific discovery, has experienced a revolution in the conduct of research. Partly because of the huge costs involved, a government contract becomes virtually a substitute for intellectual curiosity. For every old blackboard there are now hundreds of new electronic computers.[64]

Yet we must not fail to comprehend its grave implications.

Of course, Ike could not have imagined the role computers would play in the invasion of our personal privacy by internet entrepreneurial giants believing they are providing the world valuable services without realizing they are creating and opening *the* Pandora's box that can ultimately enslave humanity. As Eisenhower warned long ago, these new risks threaten losing control of our democracy and spiritual heritage.

Technology helped defeat the Nazis, and today we casually view it as constantly improving our daily lives. Instant video conferencing gives us freedom to walk down the street and communicate with anyone, at any time, anywhere around the world. But that begs the question, What will save us from technology? Are Skynet (from the *Terminator* movies), the impending reality of robots building robots, and the rapid rise of artificial intelligence all impractical fears? Will we see massive cyber warfare between these giants seeking to use their power to obtain control over our lives? Just imagine untold amounts of interdependent servers and all the software milking every single aspect of our personal data, laptops, phones, etc., for *their* use.

Ike's insightful vision of the perils of the military industrial complex could not have foretold the deep and pervasive threats of invasion of privacy of mass human activities that would follow the mail-order industry's *list builders* legacy once computers and the internet were developed. Department stores had been keeping track of my mom buying me GI Joes and underwear for a long time before computers ever became a part of the consumer market scene. The marketers knew what you would buy, where you would buy it, how often we went to each department, and if we shopped in more than one department on each visit. Even then, consumer patterns were being watched and deeply analyzed like a season of *Madmen*—albeit on less efficient index cards with scores of data entry personnel performing the tasks by hand.

Today Google performs the function of recording and analyzing every time we strike the enter key of our computer. This is a power greater than government. At least with the government, people can go with signs and banners and some of their friends and stand in front of a congressperson's office, protest, and possibly get on the evening news. Not so with a corporation, as the owners are the stockholders, dispersed all over the world, and unconcerned about your group unless it affects their pocketbook.

Everybody is frustrated about the inability to even communicate with these mega companies that have so much power and elusiveness. It's mind-blowing: A limited number of tech companies, such as Google, TikTok, Facebook, and Instagram influence many parts of our brains now, controlling the information, thoughts, and visuals that we see or don't see, or that we hear or don't hear. We understand the risk of repeating the Gilded Age, but now the stakes are far greater than just railroads and oil. Humanity is facing its greatest crossroads yet in history. Is Skynet an exaggeration . . . or a mild version of the future?

It's long been said the pen is mightier than the sword. But what happens when giant technology companies control all the pens? Eisenhower was worried the military industrial complex was the ominous threat to democracy. But now, controlling the very flow of information has become a much greater societal concern.

When there is a data breach—when our laptop, iPad, or cell phone allows our private information to become stolen or disrupted—we are threatened with losing an important component of our freedom, our privacy. We are dependent on technology. Can you imagine if we all couldn't use our phones—at all, for any reason—for days on end? No communication. No texts. No snaps. No news. No Amazon Prime. No clock. No camera. No music. All the chaotic dreams of the Joker, the Riddler, and the Penguin would become our reality!

Hardly anyone owns a ham radio anymore, and few own a television with rabbit ears. Pay phones don't exist anymore, and no one knows anyone else's phone number by memory like everyone *used* to. We've outsourced all of that—even our own brains—to the technology companies we've come to rely on.

But those "advancements" have come at a price. And the price is *high*.

Does having more personal data accessible to the governments of the world allow us to live in more freedom or force us to live in more fear? The fear of losing our freedom must be paramount against the dominance of entrepreneurial giants who conceivably have more power than the government. And more frighteningly, the government may one day control or own these massively powerful entities themselves.

The purveyors of ransomware are criminals no different than kidnappers holding our freedoms hostage. We have all read how these villains threaten our water and electrical supply, our medical systems and hospital records, and so mankind will become a prisoner of these fiends. Their goal is to essentially abduct vital operating systems from critical institutions that businesses too often cannot protect and/or the government is unwilling or unable to protect. If planes can't fly, health records are not accessible, and electricity is not flowing, you can bet the bank that more than enough people will be affected to justify group litigation.

But truly imagine if these elements control our water supply or the electrical grid, these scenarios create gigantic new vistas of future group representation actions. *Everybody* is the ultimate group; *everyone* drinks water and uses electric power, gas, sewers, down to our traffic lights and walk signals. These lawsuits make the players who are responsible for maintaining these structures, these utilities that give us our comfort, go the extra mile to protect us from these evildoers.

Or so we hope.

In the next and final chapter, we will look to the future of group representation litigation as technological giants advance, ever-new fact patterns emerge, creative development continues on blockchain and artificial intelligence, and unique devices continue to transform and threaten long-held, established core principles of American society. How will we protect ourselves from these challenges?

Chapter 19

Keeping Freedom Alive

―――――◆―――――

The arc of the moral universe is long, but it bends towards justice.
—Dr. Martin Luther King, Jr. Selma to Montgomery,
March 1965

If Coke and Bacon fought over the power of the king and Eisenhower warned us about the military industrial complex, today our concerns must focus on our privacy rights in the future and the power that data aggregators and other giants, such as Google, Facebook, Microsoft, and Apple, possess over our freedoms. Group representation once focused on a group of coal miners in Arkansas, the crew of an English privateering ship, or the Southern pastors of the nation's largest church. The future classes will be thirty million plus people vs. the present-day Goliaths.

Whenever a society is at an important crossroad, deciding which way to go will determine the future. The reality is that reining in humongous organizations cannot effectively be addressed by our imperfect democratic representative system of government. As Brian

T. Fitzpatrick masterfully argues in his *Conservative Case for Class Actions*, private sector enforcement of contracts and the prevention of fraud through group representation lawsuits is superior to governmental action, thereby lessening the role of government, lowering our taxes, and creating more directed and effective ultimate solutions. I add to this that we must be guided in the future with humanity at the center of entrepreneurship. Together these are critical tools to control these nameless, faceless, unreachable juggernaut enterprises and to hold them accountable.

HEROES

Just a few among the billions of souls that have inhabited our earth were true heroes who changed the course of history. But, as we have seen, small groups can have a long-lasting, positive impact. One person with passion can change the course of history by their example or by motivating others, sometimes without even knowing that they have done so. If our American community possesses inspired advocates on both sides, or on all sides, operating with clear humanistic rules and respect, we can create and craft the best society for future generations.

John the Tanner and his mates attempted to take on the king in 1309, standing up for all Channel Islanders and against French currency. Although they failed, their representation of everyone on the Islands set the spark of a moment that ripened into ultimate success three hundred years later.

General William West exemplified the best of America's hardworking, fighting spirit. A highly successful businessman and trusted leader throughout his community, he sacrificed everything for the creation of our American republic. His influence, like that of many other revolutionary leaders, is still felt today. Sadly, West's historical impact is remembered today more by his son's unsuccessful challenge against the father's estate than the courage and dedication that West displayed in forming our new country.

While John the Tanner had gumption and General West had impressive bravery and honor, Justice Joseph Story's greatness arose from his brilliance as a sage and scholar. While making a fortune writing law books, he dedicated himself to educating both the bar and the public about the concepts of law that remained core legal texts over the next sixty years.

Perhaps there is no better example in this book of one person taking on personal sacrifice and challenge to fight against immoral laws and making a difference than Carl Hansberry, who moved his family into a segregated Chicago neighborhood to challenge racial discrimination laws. Sadly this long-term advocate did not live to see his efforts to outlaw racially restrictive covenants realized, but again, positive change often takes time.

Thurgood Marshall is renowned as a historic legal figure for the ages. But even if an observer only studied Marshall's time as a practicing attorney limited to class actions, his record is extraordinary, by any standard of measurement, for taking on a belief system that did not serve all people equally and fairly.

Attorney Kenneth J. Mullane was court appointed to represent unknown trust beneficiaries. The famous due process case bearing his name was fought all the way to the U.S. Supreme Court after losing in both the New York trial and Supreme Court. The *Mullane* case has appeared in legal documents tens of thousands of times since it was decided. For my long experience in the "due process" business, I have seen it cited in almost every settlement agreement I was duty bound to administer. Kenneth Mullane changed every group representation beneficiary's life, and I guess, in the end, my own entrepreneurial journey.

THE FRANKPLEDGE

We have seen that long-held traditional legal practices develop and change, but they ultimately remain tethered to the past. I discussed the ancient practice of the frankpledge in chapter 2, "1199: Rector Sues His Parishioners," and the rise of the corporate entity replacing old concepts of historical group representation concepts in chapter 4, "1612: *The Case of Sutton's Hospital*." We can see that these notions and concepts remain alive today. Nowadays, most large monetary class actions, mass tort, and group representation lawsuits are, by design, against corporations. Our modern-day, centralized state policing utilizes group representation to enforce responsibility onto corporate managers, the modern-day patrol officers of the frankpledge, to protect and serve the public and to avoid corporate liability on the shareholders. Now the law and you, the consumer, stand in the place of the king and queen, holding the important role of enforcing equity. Each defined class is enforcing a twenty-first-century, restructured form of the frankpledge.

CUSTOMARY RIGHTS

We have also seen the past role of customary rights, such as the priest always coming to town to perform funeral services and everyday prayers, payments to the church of tithes, or the rights and privileges of all of those ruled by the English Crown. *Mullane* spoke of "feasible and customary substitutes" for providing notice. However, because of the rapid transformation of communication, our customs are changing as fast as our language due to data, speed, and innovations.

How are we, as Americans and part of the Western world, to keep our moral compass, our true north, our common decency, going forward? How can corporate managers maintain our customs in the face of the rapid change from postal roads to text messaging with thousands of different apps?

THE ESSENCE OF AMERICA

America was born from the idea, and General West fought for the right, that we will not be ruled by tyrants and their minions deciding the rules set by their whims, or breaking the rules, just as easily, without our consent. The American character was built on the frontier to keep developing a better society based upon the rule of law. No large landowner, employer, or corporation can act and break the rules. However, for the system to work properly, everyone certainly has both rights and responsibilities. In my view, the most important right we possess is the right to vote. Everyone's participation is critical. Because we have the privilege to vote and the right to petition the government, we also have the obligation to pay taxes (gulp) and serve on juries with our peers. The latter protects us from jaded judges who can have hardened opinions based on extended judicial service.

The essence of our country is the encouragement and acceptance of individual dreams if the dreamer complies with the laws of the group, our America. These individuals are then duly rewarded for their ingenuity and industry. But for as many people as possible to enjoy the American dream, we need maximum participation of large numbers voting, paying their taxes, serving on juries, and filling out their class action postcards or responding to group litigation emails.

POSTCARDS AND PARTICIPATION

That annoying little class action postcard. Why do I keep receiving these postcards and emails? I respond, I fill it out, and maybe receive only $20. Only the attorneys are getting rich! No! Don't complain about the postcard. Participation is the essence of America. It is easier to fill out a class action postcard than an election ballot. Indeed, how else can we have non-government oversight of unlawful corporate behavior unless the most people participate?

I admit I used to proudly boast, "I avoided jury duty." Many to most would commiserate, except for lawyers that I have met at conferences. They were genuinely enthusiastic about their role in our system and helped me fully appreciate the jury system, and everyone's duty to participate as the epitome of the role of justice that makes America great. A jury of our peers. So, like voting, paying taxes, and jury duty, *your civic duty* is to be a hero and just respond to the postcard or email. It's that easy.

If your class action involves three thousand or thirty thousand people, you might think, *Hey, I'm only one of thirty thousand and I'm only going to get a small amount. Is it worth it?* But think—it is useless to organize a group and take protest signs in front of these massive, nameless, faceless woolly mammoths, perhaps facing a similar destiny. But we can fill out the postcards, mail them in, and cause *some* financial payback, hopefully modifying corporate behavior in the future. Remember, the last place a business wants to be is at the other end of that postcard or email. They are not happy paying out those accumulated claims even if your share seems too paltry.

HUMANE TREATMENT

For our experiment in democracy to reach its full potential, we *must* teach and treat everyone humanely. To have a cohesive society and to limit the activities of bad actors, humane treatment of all must be at the core of our business ideals and ways of life. I believe that humane treatment is an important tool to counter the challenges of rapid technological change. And when we don't or can't temper the bad actors, there is hope ... the age-old cure: group representation.

Consider the lyrics from the great old-time song:

You got to ac-cent-tchu-ate the positive
E-lim-i-nate the negative
And latch on to the affirmative
Don't mess with Mr. In-between.
                   "Ac-Cent-Tchu-Ate the Positive," Johnny Mercer, 1944

Thinking and acting positively, by design, motivates humans to make more moral choices. But humanity isn't perfect. We must mess with "Mr. In-between" because of the complex world we live in. As a practical matter, as businesspeople and citizens, we can't always be totally positive and affirmative. Democracy, like all things in life, including lawsuits, requires an acceptance that nothing can be perfect or totally positive. The wise sage Winston Churchill once said, "Democracy is the worst form of government except for all those other forms that have been tried from time to time." This still rings true for group representation. With so many individuals involved, everyone cannot obtain the same degree of justice or fairness. Sheep will always stray from the flock, but group representation lawsuits continue to help keep those negative actors from wandering away from the rules that all of us must follow so business competition does not take unfair advantage of the consumer.

THE MERITS OF GROUP REPRESENTATION

The original framers could never have imagined the complexities of today's world. Due to the rapid evolutionary advancements, the very essence of America is challenged daily. How do we, as a group, as a people, control the information explosion harvested by mega corporations, overshadowing the power of the robber barons of the 1890s? Group representation can and must provide the guardrails needed to control this phenomenon. It is imperfect, as is life, but small actions can save the day.

We love participating in groups. Individuals find solace in activities such as praying together or singing the chorus of a favorite song with others. Humans are social animals. Admittedly, when we fill out the postcard, we do not *feel* part of the group. But we can. Try to feel the power of being part of the group the next time you receive that postcard or email. Your action is on the far side of that technological complexity—the simplicity of acting with a basic sense of judicial fairness and due process under law, allowing the time-tested, ageless wonder of group representation to protect our freedoms.

HUMANISTIC ENTREPRENEURSHIP

From researching and writing this book, I have come to learn that my enterprise could be called a *due process* company planted by the seeds of history, and more specifically, created by the *Mullane* decision and the 1960s wonkish class action rules. I knew I was providing the best reasonable notice, adjudicating and paying claims, providing attestation to court and counsel, and reporting to the IRS. I just had not seen the bigger picture of where I fit into this larger continuum of history.

But working on this book also made me think a lot more about, while enjoying our journey on the cyberspace highway, are we selling our data, our souls, for free, or is the Faustian bargain of exchanging our personal data 'at no cost' and forfeiting our privacy worth it? Are we sacrificing our core spiritual values for these companies' profit and power? If we are going to keep freedom alive, we need to have the whole planet working cohesively together, addressing this issue so we are in control.

Of course, as an entrepreneur, I want business to have the ability to grow and enjoy profits. Yes, I want you to have the choice to be able to construct a chemical plant. But it must also be fundamental that you can't be so unrestrained that you're destroying everybody's water and air at the same time. The essence of true freedom is basic humanity to one another, so that we are each able to be our best possible selves. And, by the same token, it's important from a business point of view that we be able to make sure our competitors are following the same rules. Without this, honest, moral entrepreneurs cannot compete because the rule breakers end up victimizing everybody: consumer, competitor, and society as a whole.

ENTREPRENEURIAL VISION

In my work of creating a superior class action administration company, I am fortunate to feel good about creating a new software platform designed for well-integrating all aspects of administering large group litigation. Everything is easy for users to find in one place. Class action administrators are the ones who read the rules of the case from the court settlement order or judgment. How many times should we resend the postcard or email? How should we attempt to contact people who don't respond? Our hardware and software applications are certainly a huge help with the economical processing of the parties to fit the case's needs, considerations such as how much reach and frequency of notice must be given each person and how to follow the court ordered guidelines on paying class members.

Group representation's future will likely employ blockchain technology (shared databases among computer networks) that will enable locating people anywhere, anytime, on any platform. Major corporations currently employ blockchain applications for financial transactions, securing personal data, voting, government benefits, and logistics and supply chain tracking. I foresee a National American

Settlement Hub being created one day that will allow anyone to find all settlements they are entitled to. Instantly findable, instantly payable. This will probably be the "feasible and customary substitute" of the future. Attorney Mullane could never have imagined this.

Consider the future impact and omnipotence of our emerging technological world. Artificial intelligence, machine learning, using metadata to search transaction records, search queries, social network interactions, and supervised learning—all of these will only expand exponentially, and they will include the development of unique algorithm detection correlation patterns linking various pieces of information that are constantly updating and improving.

Ironically, the same platforms will also be creating the megagroup representation cases of the future.

MORAL ENTREPRENEURSHIP

The goal of moral entrepreneurship is to create positive social and environmental change while also achieving financial success. Faced with this modern tech-driven reality, being a moral entrepreneur and employing business strategies and practices that promote ethical and socially responsible goals is the only way a business should operate while it also limits its exposure to being a defendant in a group representation lawsuit. This includes using environmentally friendly technologies and production methods and utilizing triple bottom line accounting by measuring a company's financial performance and its social and environmental impacts. It's about being concerned about your business's interests while also respecting the law and moral codes—the same goals as the traditional model, with different emphasis. A lofty goal, but humans all make mistakes; perfection does not exist. We are imperfect people in an imperfect world trying to create a more perfect society; we always fall short, but we must always try to do our best.

We need to allow time for reflection on the ramifications of the details of every decision we make, and hopefully the authors of our future truly consider all the different sides, teach argument and debate, and yet allow society to operate on a global scale, together. Ultimately, group litigation is a great tool for keeping balance in the business world.

When you receive the class action notification postcard or email you will no longer state, "Why am I getting this darn postcard or email?" This little postcard protects your freedom. It provides the original notice of the action, advises you of your right to opt out, or to make your claim so that you can get paid. The postcard is a metaphor for the entire group action concept. Using your voice adds protection that allows all others to stand up as well. It is a vote for or against the current issue. There was a story behind you being identified and notified by that postcard. The story will continue after you receive it. The postcard is not a burden; it as an opportunity to extend freedom, to support not only the goals of the specific case but to honor the class action heroes, the plaintiffs and defendants, the attorneys, the representatives seeking you out, the process itself, and to celebrate your part in protecting everyone via the group litigation process.

ACKNOWLEDGMENTS

There are essentially two great legal minds that provide the core guidance to allow me to create this book so that it can even exist. First is the distinguished Professor Emeritus at UCLA School of Law School Stephen Yeazell, the author of *From Medieval Group Litigation to the Modern Class Action*, the seminal scholarly treatise about the history of group representation and class actions through the ages. His fine volume provided the extensive, in-depth historical outline of the key cases and concepts of law that guided me throughout this entire undertaking. Without his fine scholarship, my 'storybook' would have been an impossible mountain to climb.

Second, my ghostwriter, Joel Bander, an accomplished attorney with twenty-five years of litigation experience, including many successful class actions. I first met Mr. Bander when marketing my class action administration company in the mid-1990s and we became fast friends. After years of working together, more off than on, I proposed the idea of a class action history book to him knowing he would be the perfect collaborator. I discovered that we shared a profound interest in history. He methodically outlined the chapters, and utilizing his special knowledge of the merger of law and its relation to the historical times brought insight into areas I never had previously thought about or considered. Bander then required me to tell the story in my own words, and we would then collaborate on how to enrich each tale.

Third, I am grateful for Ashley Jensen for taking the time to creatively illustrate this book and bring the visuals to life. Thanks for thirty eight years of working together.

Additionally, I would like to thank Michael Macintosh, a class action administration pioneer, who educated me about the history of skip tracing, the art of finding lost people critical to the industry, which was critical to the last section of the book.

Of course, my parents, Dr. William Arthur Hoffman & Deborah Apgar Hoffman, who ever since I was young always instilled the importance and unique dynamic of learning, experiencing and appreciating history and how much it impacts our lives every day. It seems they brought my brother Zach and me to every possible historical museum, from the mundane, the First Home Airconditioning Museum, to the extraordinary, Edison Ford Museum in Fort Myers, Florida, where two great entrepreneurs would collaborate. Among the countless places they took us that spurred my interest in history were the Alamo, Fort Sumter, medieval village recreations, and perhaps most notable, the Texas State Railroad Palestine Depot, where we got to ride on vintage trains, including the Presidential Couch, and truly felt we were living in the past.

Finally, to my grandmother, Ann Hoffman, a journalist who interviewed two sitting presidents, wrote for newspapers and major national magazines and penned her own books while also building a large clothing company from New Jersey to South Florida. She would make me sit and read with her in history books, of which Richard Nixon's on leadership, and the autobiography on Armand Hammer having a profound impact on my interest in history and my long-term professional direction. From there I never stopped reading, listening to and visiting every place of history I possibly could.

ENDNOTES

CHAPTER 1
1606–1616: WHEN THE KING SAVED EQUITY

1. Thomas Longueville, *The Curious Case of Lady Purbeck, A Scandal of the XVIIth Century*: March 4, 2005 (EBook #15257).
2. Ibid.
3. Charles E. Shepard, "Coke and Bacon: A Study of Character," *American Bar Association Journal*, Vol. 11, No. 5 (May 1925): 333–336.
4. Ibid.
5. Alan Stewart, *The Cradle King: A Life of James VI & I* (Macmillan, 2003); "George Villiers, 1st Duke of Buckingham," Wikipedia.org, https://en.wikipedia.org/wiki/George_Villiers,_1st_Duke_of_Buckingham #CITEREFStewart2003.
6. John Baker, "Coke's Note-Books and the Sources of His Reports," *Cambridge Law Journal*. (1): 59–86.
7. Sir Edward Coke, *The Reports of Sir Edward Coke, Knt.*, 13 vols. (London, 1572–1617).
8. "Elizabeth Hatton," Wikipedia.org, https://en.wikipedia.org/wiki/Elizabeth_Hatton; "Sir Edward Coke (Lord Chief Justice, 1613–16)," *The Diary of Samuel Pepys*, https://www.pepysdiary.com/encyclopedia/8409/.

CHAPTER 3
1309: THE FIRST JUDICIALLY CREATED CONSUMER CLASS ACTION

9. Raymond B. Marcin, "Searching for the Origin of Class Action," *Catholic University Law Review* 23 (1974), 515, 522.
10. Ibid.
11. *Devyke v. Petevyn*, Acta Cancellariae or Selections from the Records of the Court of Chancery, No. LX, at 369 (1847); Reg. Lib. A., 1566, 1567, fo. 80, 23 Catholic University Law Review 515, 524.
12. *Catholic University Law Review* 23, (1974), 515, 524.

CHAPTER 4
1612: *CASE OF SUTTON'S HOSPITAL*

13. Francis Bacon, *Novum Organum* (1620).

CHAPTER 5
1676: *BROWN V. VERMUDEN*— BINDING ABSENT PARTIES

14. Katherine J. Wu, "The Fallout of a Medieval Archbishop's Murder Is Recorded in Alpine Ice," *Smithsonian Magazine*, April 2, 2020, https://www.smithsonianmag.com/smart-news/researchers-find-fallout-medieval-archbishops-murder-recorded-alpine-ice-180974565/.
15. Edward Grim, "The Martyrdom of St. Thomas Becket," Simply Catholic, https://www.simplycatholic.com/martyrdom-of-thomas-becket/.
16. Ben Johnson, "The Great Plague 1665," Historic UK, https://www.historic-uk.com/HistoryUK/HistoryofEngland/The-Great-Plague/#:~:text=80%25%20of%20the%20people%20died,plague%20had%20run%20its%20course.

CHAPTER 6
1762: A LICENSE TO WAGE WAR

17. *Chancey v. May*, 24 Eng. Rep. 265 (Ch. 1722).
18. *Good v. Blewitt*, 33 Eng. Rept 343, 345 (Ch. 1807).

CHAPTER 7
1820: GENERAL WEST AND THE LICENTIOUS REPUBLIC

19. *West v. Randall*, 29 F. Cas. 718, 721 (C.C.D.R.I. 1820) (Story, J.).
20. Ibid.
21. C. C. Beaman, "An Historical Address delivered in Scituate, Rhode Island, July 4, 1876, at the request of the town authorities" (1877). Rhode Island History. 16. https://rihistoriccemeteries.org/newsearchcemeterydetail.aspx?ceme_no=SC026.
22. Providence Public Library, *James Newell Arnold Collection*, ca. 1880–1927, Mss. 029-02, Providence, Rhode Island.

CHAPTER 8
1820–1845: JOSEPH STORY TEACHING AMERICA EQUITY

23. Calvin Woodard, *Joseph Story and American Equity*, 45 Wash. & Lee L. Rev. 623, 630 (1988), https://scholarlycommons.law.wlu.edu/wlulr/vol45/iss2/7.
24. Ibid.
25. Alexander Hamilton, Federalist Paper 83.
26. *The Amistad*, 40 U.S. 518, 558, 10 L. Ed. 826 (1841), https://www.archives.gov/education/lessons/amistad.
27. Ibid.
28. Woodard, *Joseph Story and American Equity*, 632.
29. Joseph Story, *Commentaries on Equity Jurisprudence*, 1st ed. (1836), § 59.
30. Woodard, *Joseph Story and American Equity*, 623, 632.
31. Joseph Story, *Commentaries on Equity Pleading*, sec. 120.

CHAPTER 9
1845: *SMITH V. SWORMSTEDT*—THE SOUTH SECEDES

32. Alexis de Tocqueville, *Democracy in America* (1835).
33. Geoffrey Hazard, John L. Gedid, and Stephen Sowie, "An Historical Analysis of the Binding Nature of Class Suits," Faculty Scholarship, Paper 1423. 1901 (1998).

34. Phillip Stone, "How the Methodist Church Split in the 1840s," *From the Archives*, Wofford College Blogs, January 30, 2013
35. *Smith v. Swormstedt* 57 U.S. 288, 296, 300 (1853).
36. *Smith*, supra, 302.
37. Ibid. 298.

CHAPTER 10
1920: THE TRIBE OF BEN-HUR

38. "Ulysses S. Grant: The Myth of 'Unconditional Surrender' Begins at Fort Donelson," American Battlefield Trust, https://www.battlefields.org/learn/articles/ulysses-s-grant-myth-unconditional-surrender-begins-fort-donelson.
39. Jason Strykowski, "An Unholy Bargain in a Cursed Place: Lew Wallace, William Bonney, and New Mexico Territory, 1878–1881," *New Mexico Historical Review* 82, 2 (2007).
40. Federal Practice - Class Suits - Community of Interest Under Federal Equity Rule 38, 30 *Michigan Law Review* 624 (1932).
41. *Supreme Tribe of Ben Hur v. Cauble*, 255 U.S. 356, 366 (1921).
42. Ibid.

CHAPTER 11
1905–1925: GILDED AGE UNION WARS

43. *Pettibone v. Nichols*, 203 U.S. 192, 218 (1906).
44. *Goldfield Consol. Mines Co. v. Goldfield Miners' Union No. 220*, 159 F. 500 (1908).
45. *United Mine Workers of America v. Coronado Coal Co.*, 259 U.S. 344 (1922).

CHAPTER 12
1936: THE BIRTH OF GRANDFATHER 23

46. James Wm. Moore, "Federal Rules of Civil Procedure: Some Problems Raised by the Preliminary Draft," *Georgetown Law Journal* 25, no. 3 (March 1937): 551–576.

47. James Wm. Moore, "Federal Rules of Civil Procedure: Some Problems Raised by the Preliminary Draft," *Georgetown Law Journal* 25 (1937), 551.

CHAPTER 13
1940–1950: DUE PROCESS TRUMPS RACIALLY RESTRICTIVE COVENANTS

48. *Lee v. Hansberry*, 372 Ill. 369, 373 (1939).
49. Ibid. 379.

CHAPTER 14
1954: *BROWN V. BOARD OF EDUCATION*

50. *Brown v. Board of Ed. of Topeka, Shawnee County, Kan.*, 347 U.S. 483 (1954).
51. NCC Staff, "Looking Back at the Brown v. Board Decision," Constitution Daily Blog (National Constitution Center), November 23, 2015, https://constitutioncenter.org/blog/looking-back-at-the-decision-that-ended-segregation.
52. *Kansas City v. Williams*, 205 F.2d 47 (8th Cir. 1953).
53. Kim Barbieri, "Ike's Second Term as President," *The Eisenhower Life Series: Called to a Higher Duty*, Eisenhower Foundation, 2002, https://eisenhowerfoundation.net/ikes-life/ikes-second-term-president
54. *Kansas City v. Williams*, 205 F.2d 47 (8th Cir. 1953).
55. Juan Williams, "Thurgood Marshall, American Revolutionary," American Heritage, Winter 2020, https://www.americanheritage.com/thurgood-marshall-american-revolutionary.
56. Nathan T. Prewett, "Panel at Birmingham Public Library to discuss George Wallace," AL.com, September 5, 2013, https://www.al.com/living/2013/09/panel_at_birmingham_public_lib.html.
57. Harrison Smith, Ellie Silverman, "Linda Brown Thompson, girl at center of *Brown v. Board of Education* case, dies," *Washington Post*, March 26, 2018.

CHAPTER 15
1961: THE ONE-WAY INTERVENTION CONTROVERSY

58. "Federal Courts—Procedure—Nonlitigating Members of 'Spurious' Class May Intervene After Verdict to Share in Damages," *Harvard Law Review* 76 (1963): 1675, 1678.

CHAPTER 16
1966: THE YEAR EVERYTHING CHANGED

59. Rye Murphy, "Competing Ideologies at the Formation of the Federal Class Action Rule: Legal Process Versus Legal Liberalism," *Drexel Law Review* 10, no. 2 (2018): 389–444, https://drexel.edu/~/media/Files/law/law%20review/v10-2/Murphy%2010%20Drexel%20L%20Rev%20389.ashx.
60. David Marcus, "Flawed But Noble: Desegregation Litigation and its Implications for the Modern Class Action," Arizona Legal Studies Discussion Paper No. 10-32 (forthcoming in *Florida Law Review*), posted September 17, 2010, SSRN scholarly paper 1678803, https://papers.ssrn.com/sol3/papers.cfm?abstract_id=1678803.
61. David Marcus, "Flawed But Noble

CHAPTER 17
THE WORLD OF GROUP LITIGATION— PROLOGUE TO THE FUTURE

62. Andrew N. Case, "'The solid gold mailbox': direct mail and the changing nature of buying and selling in the postwar United States," History of Retailing and Consumption, 1:1, 28-4 (2015).

CHAPTER 18
FREEDOM THREATENED

63. Tim Rives, "'OK, We'll Go': Just What Did Ike Say When He Launched the D-day Invasion 70 Years Ago?" Archives.gov, https://www.archives.gov/files/publications/prologue/2014/spring/d-day.pdf.
64. "President Dwight D. Eisenhower's Farewell Address (1961), National Archives, https://www.archives.gov/milestone-documents/president-dwight-d-eisenhowers-farewell-address.

BIBLIOGRAPHY

CHAPTER 1
1606–1616: WHEN THE KING SAVED EQUITY

Stephen C. Yeazell, *From Medieval Group Litigation to the Modern Class Action*, Yale University Press (1987).

Thomas Longueville, *The Curious Case of Lady Purbeck: A Scandal of the XVIIth Century*, March 4, 2005. Project Gutenberg eBook #15257.

Charles E. Shepard, "Coke and Bacon A Study of Character," *American Bar Association Journal* 11 (1925): 333 .

Alan Stewart, *The Cradle King: A Life of James VI & I*. Macmillan, 2003.

Wikipedia. "George Villiers, 1st Duke of Buckingham." Last modified [date]. Accessed [date]. https://en.wikipedia.org/wiki/George_Villiers,_1st_Duke_of_Buckingham#CITEREFStewart2003

R. A. MacKay, "Coke: Parliamentary Sovereignty or the Supremacy of the Law?" *Michigan Law Rev* 22 (1924): 218.

John Baker, "Coke's Note-Books and the Sources of His Reports." *Cambridge Law Journal* (1972).

Wikipedia. "Elizabeth Hatton." Last modified [date]. Accessed [date]. https://en.wikipedia.org/wiki/Elizabeth_Hatton.

Samuel Pepys. *The Diary of Samuel Pepys*. Accessed [date]. https://www.pepysdiary.com/encyclopedia/8409/.

Francis Watt. "Lord Coke as a Person." *Juridical Review* 27 (1915): 250.

"Coke and Bacon: The Conservative Lawyer, and the Law Reformer." *American Law Review* 31 (1897): 1.

David W. Raack. "A History of Injunctions in England Before 1700." *Indiana Law Journal* 61, no. 4 (1986): Article 1.

Audrey Marie Cline. *An Analysis of the Essay, Lord Bacon, by Lord Macaulay, with the Purpose of Revealing Early Victorian Values.* Seminar Paper, Wisconsin State University, 1967.

W. S. Holdsworth. "The Early History of Equity." *Michigan Law Review* 13, no. 4 (February 1915).

James Spielman. "Lions in Conflict: Ellesmere, Bacon, and Coke—The Prerogative Battles." *Australian Bar Review* (December 2013).

Howard L. Oleck. "Historical Nature of Equity Jurisprudence." *Fordham Law Review* 20 (1951): 23.

CHAPTER 2
1199: RECTOR SUES HIS PARISHIONERS

Barkway Church. *St. Mary Magdalene, Barkway Church Guide.* Barkway Church, n.d.

Norma Adams and Charles Donahue. *Select Cases from the Ecclesiastical Courts of the Province of Canterbury c. 1200–1301.* Selden Society, 1981.

Georgene Vairo. "What Goes Around, Comes Around: From the Rector of Barkway to Knowles." *The Review of Litigation* 32 (2013): 721.

Nicholas Tuflon. Email correspondence with the author, 2020.

Susan T. Spence. "Looking Back . . . In a Collective Way: A Short History of Class Action Law." *Business Law Today* 11, no. 6 (July/August 2002).

Geoffrey Hazard, John L. Gedid, and Stephen Sowie. "An Historical Analysis of the Binding Nature of Class Suits." *University of Pennsylvania Law Review* 146 (1998): 1849.

CHAPTER 3
1309: THE FIRST JUDICIALLY CREATED CONSUMER CLASS ACTION

Raymond Marcin. "Searching for the Origin of Class Action." *Catholic University Law Review* 23 (1974): 515.

Devyke v. Petevyn, Acta Cancellariae or Selections from the Records of the Court of Chancery, No. LX, at 369 Reg. Lib. A., 1566 (1847).

William Craddock Bolland. *Select Bills in Eyre, 1282–1333.* 2009.

Girart Dorens. "Sir Otho de Grandison 1238?–1328." *Transactions of the Royal Historical Society* (1909).

H. G. Keene. "The Channel Islands." *The English Historical Review*, January 1887.

Henry Treece. *The Crusades.* Barnes & Noble, 1962.

CHAPTER 4
1612: *CASE OF SUTTON'S HOSPITAL*

Francis Bacon. *Novum Organum.* 1620.

Mark Knights. "Impeachment: A Political Weapon That Went Out of Fashion in England Just as It Was Adopted in the US." *The Conversation.* January 30, 2020.

A. D. Innes. "The Duke of Buckingham and Sir Francis Bacon." *A History of the British Nation.* T.C. & E.C. Jack, 1912.

Impeachment in the Early Seventeenth Century. The History of Parliament.

James I and the Duke of Buckingham: Love, Power and Betrayal. The History of Parliament.

Parliaments, 1604–1629: The Reigns of James I and Charles I. The History of Parliament Online.

Damian X. Powell. "Why Was Sir Francis Bacon Impeached? The Common Lawyers and the Chancery Revisited: 1621." Accessed at https://www.jstor.org/stable/24422782.

Frank O. Bowman III. "British Impeachments (1376–1787) and the Preservation of the American Constitutional Order." *Hastings Constitutional Law Quarterly* 46 (2019): 745.

The Case of Sutton's Hospital. Michaelmas Term, 10 James I (1612).

Steve Sheppard, ed. *The Selected Writings and Speeches of Sir Edward Coke, Volume One.* Liberty Fund, 2003.

Stephen C. Yeazell. "Group Litigation and Social Context: Toward a History of the Class Action." *Columbia Law Review* 77 (1977): 866.

Theodore Dwight. "Trial by Impeachment." *American Law Register*, 1867.

CHAPTER 5
1676: *BROWN V. VERMUDEN*—
BINDING ABSENT PARTIES

Katherine J. Wu. "The Fallout of a Medieval Archbishop's Murder Is Recorded in Alpine Ice." *Smithsonian Magazine*, April 2, 2020.

"The Martyrdom of St. Thomas Becket." *Simply Catholic.* Accessed at https://www.simplycatholic.com/martyrdom-of-thomas-becket/.

The Great Plague. Historic UK. Accessed at https://www.historic-uk.com/HistoryUK/HistoryofEngland/The-Great-Plague/#:~:text=80%25%20of%20the%20people%20died,plague%20had%20run%20its%20course.

Chancey v. May, 24 Eng. Rep. 265 (Ch. 1722).

Good v. Blewitt, 33 Eng. Rep. 343 (Ch. 1807).

"Air Pollution from 12th Century British Lead Mines Has Been Detected in the Swiss Alps." *Daily Mail Online*, May 7, 2020.

Christopher P. Loveluck. "Alpine Ice and the Annual Political Economy of the Angevin Empire, from the Death of Thomas Becket to Magna Carta, c. AD 1170–1216." *Antiquity* 94, no. 374 (2020).

Donald Fleming and Bernard Bailyn, eds. *Perspectives in American History, Volume V: Law in American History.* Charles Warren Center for Studies in American History, Harvard University, 1971.

Howard L. Oleck. "Historical Nature of Equity Jurisprudence." *Fordham Law Review* 20 (1951): 23.

Katherine J. Wu. "The Fallout of a Medieval Archbishop's Murder Is Recorded in Alpine Ice." *Smithsonian Magazine,* April 2, 2020.

Brown v. Vermuden, 1 Ch. Cas. 272, 22 Eng. Rep. 796 (1676).

Stephen C. Yeazell. "Group Litigation and Social Context: Toward a History of the Class Action." *Columbia Law Review* 77 (1977): 866.

CHAPTER 6
1762: A LICENSE TO WAGE WAR

Leigh v. Thomas, 28 Eng. Rep. 201 (1751).

Adair v. New River Company, 32 Eng. Rep. 1153 (1805).

Chancey v. May, 24 Eng. Rep. 265 (1722).

Good v. Blewitt." 33 Eng. Rept 343, 345 (1807).

William Jessop. *Privateering in Elizabethan Bristol: A Case Study,* John Hopkins. Dissertation (2004).

Henning Hillmann and Christina Gathmann. "Overseas Trade and the Decline of Privateering." *The Journal of Economic History* 71, no. 3 (September 2011).

Bryan Mabee, "Pirates, Privateers and the Political Economy of Private Violence." *Global Change, Peace & Security,* 21, no. 2, (2009).

Gary M. Anderson and Adam Gifford, Jr. "Privateering and the Private Production of Naval Power." *Cato Journal,* 11, no. 1 (Spring/Summer 1991).

Alexander Tabarrok, "The Rise, Fall, and Rise Again of Privateers." *The Independent Review,* 11, no. 3 (Winter 2007).

David Douglas, *The Trade of Bristol in The Eighteenth Century,* Bristol Record Society, 1957.

Stephen C. Yeazell, "The Past and Future of Defendant and Settlement Classes in Collective Litigation." *Arizona Law Review,* 1987.

CHAPTER 7
1820: GENERAL WEST AND THE LICENTIOUS REPUBLIC

Steven Park, *The Burning of His Majesty's Schooner* Gaspee. Westholme Publishing, 2016.

Paul A. W. Wallace, "Historic Hope Lodge." *The Pennsylvania Magazine of History and Biography,* 1962.

Beaman, C.C., "An Historical Address delivered in Scituate, Rhode Island, July 4th, 1876, at the request of the town authorities." *Rhode Island History,* 1877.

George M. West. *William West of Scituate, R.I.* Panama City Publishing Co., 1919.

James N. Arnold Collection, Number 029-02, Providence Public Library, circa 1860-1935.

Joel A. Cohen, ed. Rhode Island History, Rhode Island Historical Preservation Commission, Historical and Architectural Resources of Scituate, Rhode Island, A Preliminary Report, (1980).

West v. Randall, 29 F. Cas. 718 (C.C.D.R.I. 1820)

Cemetery SC026 in Rhode Island Historical Cemetery Commission Database.

CHAPTER 8
1820–1845: JOSEPH STORY TEACHING AMERICA EQUITY

Calvin Woodard, Joseph Story and American Equity, 45 Wash. & Lee L. Rev. 623, (1988).

Alexander Hamilton, Federalist Paper 83.

The Amistad, 40 U.S. 518 (1841).

Calvin Woodard, Joseph Story and American Equity, 45 Wash. & Lee L. Rev. 623 (1988).

Francis Tracy Carlton, The History and Problems of Organized Labor, D.C. Heath & Co. (1911).

Joseph Story, Story's Commentaries on Equity Pleading, C.C. Little and J. Brown (1838).

Joseph Story, Story's Commentaries on Equity Jurisprudence, Billard, Gray & Company (1839).

VanBurkleo, Sandra F., "Book Review: Supreme Court Justice Joseph Story: Statesman of the Old Republic. by R. Kent Newmyer." Constitutional Commentary, Uni. of Minn. Law Review (1986).

Stanley N. Katz, The Politics of Law in Colonial America: Controversies over Chancery Courts and Equity Law in the Eighteenth Century, Charles Warren Center in American History (1971).

CHAPTER 9
1845: *SMITH V. SWORMSTEDT*—THE SOUTH SECEDES

Alexis de Tocqueville, Democracy in America, Volumes One and Two, trans. Henry Reeve, the Pennsylvania State University, Electronic Classics Series, (2002).

Arthur R. Miller, The American Class Action: From Birth to Maturity, 19 Theoretical Inquiries L. 1 (2018).

Hazard, Geoffrey; Gedid, John L.; and Sowie, Stephen, "An Historical Analysis of the Binding Nature of Class Suits" (1998). Faculty Scholarship. Paper 1423. (Uni. of PA Law School).

https://christianhistoryinstitute.org/magazine/article/broken-churches-broken-nation

https://en.wikipedia.org/wiki/Methodist_Episcopal_Church,_South#:~:text=The%20Methodist%20Episcopal%20Church%2C%20South,Methodist%20Episcopal%20Church%20(MEC).

Phillip Stone, How the Methodist Church split in the 1840s, SC United Methodist Advocate, (2013).

Allen Carden Religious Schism as A Prelude to the American Civil War: Methodists, Baptists, and Slavery, Andrews University Press. (1986).

Raymond B. Marcin, Searching for the Origin of Class Action, 23 Cath. U. L. Rev. 515 (1974).

Rowe, Rebecca, "The Beginning of the End: A Look at the Causes of the Schism in the Methodist Episcopal Church" Undergraduate Research Awards. (2013).

Lawrence, Brian D., "The relationship between the Methodist church, slavery and politics, 1784-1844 Theses and Dissertations. Rowan University (2018).

Smith v. Swormstedt, 57 U.S. 288 (1853).

https://blogs.wofford.edu/from_the_archives/2013/01/30/how-the-methodist-church-split-in-the-1840s/#:~:text=Bishop%20Andrew%20explained%20that%20first,would%20permit.%E2%80%9D%20The%20young%20woman

CHAPTER 10
1920: THE TRIBE OF BEN-HUR

Federal Practice - Class Suits - Community of Interest Under Federal Equity Rule 38, 30 Mich. L. Rev. 624 (1932).

Charles Donelan, Prerequisites to a Class Action Under New Rule 23, Boston College Industrial and Commercial Law Review (1969).

https://www.battlefields.org/learn/articles/ulysses-s-grant-myth-unconditional-surrender-begins-fort-donelson

Strykowski, Jason. "An Unholy Bargain in a Cursed Place: Lew Wallace, William Bonney, and New Mexico Territory, 1878–1881." New Mexico Historical Review 82, 2 (2007).

Federal Practice - Class Suits - Community of Interest Under Federal Equity Rule 38, 30 Mich. L. Rev. 624 (1932).

Supreme Tribe of Ben Hur v. Cauble, 255 U.S. 356 (1921).

Robert E. Morsberger and Katherine M Morsberger, Lew Wallace Militant Romantic. McGraw Hill (1980).

James Madison, Jane Hedeen, and Lee Ann Sandweiss, Hoosiers and the American Story, Indiana Historical Society Press (2014).

Schmidt, Alvin J. *Fraternal Organizations* Westport, CT; Greenwood Press (1980)

https://nationalheritagemuseum.typepad.com/library_and_archives/supreme-tribe-of-ben-hur/

Kasey Greer,The Inner Battle of the Civil War: An Analysis of General Lew Wallace's Views on Slavery, Indiana University, Open Source Scholarship.

CHAPTER 11
1905–1925: GILDED AGE UNION WARS

Sidney Lens, The Labor Wars, From the Molly Maguires to the Sitdowns, Anchor Books, (1973).

https://isb.idaho.gov/wp-content/uploads/The_Crime_of_the_Century_1949.pdf

[author?]Department of Commerce and Labor, Statistics for Nevada, Thirteenth Census of the United States Taken in the Year 1910, U.S. Department of Commerce and Labor (1910).

Samuel A. Sizer, "This is Union Man's Country" Sebastian County 1914, Arkansas Historical Association, Vol. 27, No.4 (1968).

Coronado Coal Co. v. United Mine Workers of America, 268 U.S. 295 (1925).

Goldfield Consol. Mines Co. v. Goldfield Miners' Union No. 220, 159 F. 500 (1908).

United Mine Workers of America v. Coronado Coal Co., 259 U.S. 344 (1922).

Francis Bowes Sayre, Labor and the Courts, 39 Yale L. J. 682 (1930).

[Comment, no author stated] The Coronado Coal Case, 32 Yale L. J. 59 (1922).

American Steel & Wire Co. v. Wire Drawers' & Die Makers' Unions. 90 F. 598 (N.D. Ohio 1898).

O. L. Clark, Application of the Sherman Anti-Trust Act to Unions since the Apex Case, 2 Sw L.J. 94 (1948).

Milton Hirsch, Big Bill Haywood's Revenge: The Original Intent of The Exclusionary Rule 22 St. Thomas L. Rev. 35 (2009).

Milton Handler William C. Zifchak Collective Bargaining and the Antitrust Laws: The Emasculation of the Labor Exemption 81 Colum. L. Rev. 459 (1981).

Florence Peterson, Strikes in the United States 1880 -1936, U.S. Department of Labor (1937).

[Note] Labor Activity and The Antitrust Laws: A Need For Flexibility, 36 Wash. & Lee L. Rev. 1239 (1979),

Bernard D. Meltzer, Labor Unions, Collective Bargaining, And the Antitrust Laws, 32 U Chi. L. Rev. 659 (1964).

[Note} Legal Status of Voluntary Associations, 33 Harv. L. Rev. 298 (1919).

Hon. Bryon J. Johnson, No Habeas Corpus for "Big Bill", The Advocate (2006).

Jeffrey R. Boyle, The Crime of the Century, Idaho Legal History Society.

Wesley A. Sturges Unincorporated Associations as Parties to Actions, 33 Yale L. J. 383 (1924).

Pettibone v. Nichols, 203 U.S. 192 (1906).

CHAPTER 12
1936: THE BIRTH OF GRANDFATHER 23

James Wm. Moore, Federal Rules of Civil Procedure: Some Problems Raised by The Preliminary Draft 25 Georgetown Law Journal 551 (1937).

John G. Harkins, Jr. Federal Rule 23-The Early Years, 39 Ariz. L. Rev. 705 (1997).

[Note] The Spurious Class Suit: Procedural and Practical Problems Confronting Court and Counsel 53 Nw. U. L. Rev. 627 (1958).

Daniel S. Holt, From Conformity to Uniformity: The Rules Enabling Act of 1934 and the Rise of Federal Judicial Authority, The Federal Lawyer, (May 2012).

CHAPTER 13
1940–1950: DUE PROCESS TRUMPS RACIALLY RESTRICTIVE COVENANTS

Lorraine Hansberry, A Raisin in the Sun, Vintage Books (1958).

[Note] Accounting For Common Trust Funds: A Statutory Scheme 64 Harv. L. Rev. 473 (1951).

[Note] Effect of Judgment In Prior Class Suit, 49 Yale L.J. 1125 (1940).

Allen R. Kamp, The History Behind *Handsberry v. Lee*, 20 U.C. Davis L. Rev. (1987).

Lee v. Hansberry, 24 N.E.2d 37 (Ill. 1939).

Mullane v. Central Hanover Bank & Trust Co., 339 U.S. 306 (1950).

CHAPTER 14
1954: *BROWN V. BOARD OF EDUCATION*

Brown v. Board of Ed. of Topeka, Shawnee County, Kan., 347 U.S. 483 (1954).

Brown v. Board of Educ. of Topeka, Kan., 349 U.S. 294 (1955).

Chambers v. State of Florida, 309 U.S. 227 (1940).

David Marcus, Flawed but Noble: Desegregation Litigation and Its Implications For The Modern Class Action 63 Fla. L. Rev. 657 (2011).

Harrison Smith, Ellie Silverman, Linda Brown Thompson, Girl at Center of Brown v. Board of Education Case, Dies, Washington Post (March 26, 2018).

Kansas City v. Williams, 205 F.2d 47 (8th Cir. 1953).

https://library.cscc.edu/ThurgoodMarshall/Cases

https://www.theatlantic.com/magazine/archive/2015/10/thurgood-marshall-badass/403189/?gclid=Cj0KCQjw-O35BRDVARIsAJU5mQUkpBvoxIfrypsMHeTDVp6RUbZGCA1pOsgzwii-1KLVtOs4camnSMYaAth1EALw_wcB

Carlton F.W. Larson, What If Chief Justice Fred Vinson Had Not Died Of a Heart Attack In 1953?: Implications For Brown And Beyond, 45 Indiana L. Rev. 131 (2011).

https://www.americanheritage.com/thurgood-marshall-american-revolutionary

https://www.al.com/living/2013/09/panel_at_birmingham_public_lib.html

CHAPTER 15
1961: THE ONE-WAY INTERVENTION CONTROVERSY

Developments In the Law—Multiparty Litigation In Federal Courts 71 Harv. L. Rev. 877 (1958).

Federal Courts—Procedure—Nonlitigating Members of "Spurious" Class May Intervene After Verdict to Share In,76 Harv. L. Rev. 1675 (1963).

Union Carbide & Carbon Corp. v. Nisley, 300 F.2d 561 (10th Cir. 1961).

CHAPTER 16
1966: THE YEAR EVERYTHING CHANGED

https://en.wikipedia.org/wiki/Dean_Acheson

https://en.wikipedia.org/wiki/Benjamin_Kaplan

https://en.wikipedia.org/wiki/Albert_Sacks

https://en.wikipedia.org/wiki/Charles_Alan_Wright

https://en.wikipedia.org/wiki/John_Paul_Frank

Rye Murphy Competing Ideologies at The Formation of The Federal Class Action Rule: Legal Process versus Legal Liberalism 10 Drexel L. Rev. 389 (2018).

Excerpts From the Tape of The May 1966 Meeting of The Advisory Committee On Civil Rules (May 20-21, 1966).

David Marcus Flawed but Noble: Desegregation Litigation and Its Implications For The Modern Class Action, 63 Fla. L. Rev. 657 (2011).

David B. Wilkins in Memoriam: Albert M. Sacks 105 Harv. L. Rev. 20 (1991).

Brian T. Fitzpatrick The Ironic History of Rule 23 Vanderbilt University Law School (2017).

Allan Ryan Judgments On Nuremberg: The Past Half Century And Beyond—A Panel Discussion Of Nuremberg Prosecutors 16 B.C. Third World L.J. 193 (1966).

David Marcus, The History of The Modern Class Action, Part I: Sturm Und Drang, 1953—1980 90 Wash. U. L. Rev. 587 (2013).

CHAPTER 17
THE WORLD OF GROUP LITIGATION—
PROLOGUE TO THE FUTURE

Joseph Story. *Commentaries on the Constitution of the United States: With a Preliminary Review of the Constitutional History of the Colonies and States Before the Adoption of the Constitution.* 4th ed. Boston: Little, Brown and Company, 1873.

Andrew N. Case. "'The Solid Gold Mailbox': Direct Mail and the Changing Nature of Buying and Selling in the Postwar United States." *History of Retailing and Consumption* 1, no. 1 (2015): 28–44.

Virgil Eugene Harder. *A History of Direct Mail Advertising.* Thesis, University of Illinois, 1958.

Henry F. and Katharine Pringle. "Sixty Million Headaches Every Year." *The Saturday Evening Post.*

Skip Tracing Manual 2018. https://ia801008.us.archive.org/23/items/Skip TracingManual2018/Skip%20Tracing%20Manual%202018.pdf.

Troy Hoffman. Conversations with Michael McIntosh, April–May 2022.

Eugene F. Tyson. *Tested Collection Methods and Procedures.* McGraw-Hill Book Company, 1966.

William Luftig. *Credit Cheaters: A Manual on Skip Tracing Technique and Procedure.* Business Information Service Bureau, 1932.

E. H. Barnes. *Barnes on Credit and Collection.* Prentice Hall, 1961.

CHAPTER 18
FREEDOM THREATENED

Tim Rives. "Just What Did Ike Say When He Launched the D-Day Invasion 70 Years Ago?" *Prologue,* Spring 2014. Accessed at https://www.archives.gov/files/publications/prologue/2014/spring/d-day.pdf.

President Dwight D. Eisenhower's Farewell Address. National Archives. Accessed at https://www.archives.gov/milestone-documents/president-dwight-d-eisenhowers-farewell-address.

Mullane v. Central Hanover Bank & Trust Co., 339 U.S. 306 (1950).

CHAPTER 19
KEEPING FREEDOM ALIVE

Brian T. Fitzpatrick, *The Conservative Case for Class Action,* University of Chicago Press, (2019).